Fast Phonics
Testimonials

With this method, my 3 ½-year-old learned all of her phonetic sounds in 4 days! And she retained them perfectly thereafter!

(Anne Green, mother of 3, Colorado)

My grandson did the cartoon letters in the car as I drove him to private school. When we arrived there, he wanted to CONTINUE practicing his phonics cartoons RATHER than go into his schoolroom! He's hooked!

(Mrs. F., grandmother of 9, Colorado)

Our first attempt at reading—using someone else's phonics program—came to a screeching halt. My daughter hated "learning to read." With this new approach her interest not only revived, she actually sat up and took ownership. She is now six and is teaching the cartoon letters to her four-year-old brother!

(Mrs. H., mother of 4, New Mexico)

My older daughter of 6, when watching her younger sibling learn phonics with Mrs. Ellison's system, burst out with "Mom, if you had taught ME to read this way, I would have become a better reader!"

(Mrs. C., mother of 3, North Carolina)

The cartoon phonics system has been a blessing to our family. Because of the imagery connected with each letter, we were able to introduce phonics to our four-year-old and our two-year-old **at the same time**!

(Mrs. A, mother of 3, New Mexico)

Fast Phonics is FUN!

kite

ladder

mountain

nose

...want to know the secret?

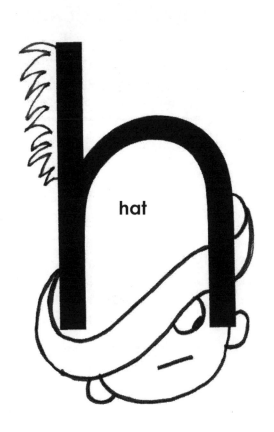

hat

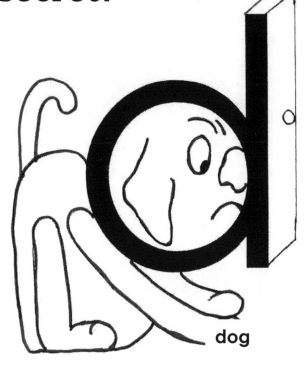

dog

The phonetic SOUND is tucked into the letter SHAPE!

give

The results?

Lasting retention, right from the start.

6 reasons why *Fast Phonics* is more effective, more fun and more rapidly acquired than traditional phonics methods:

1

Fast Phonics gets the child **READING RIGHT NOW** (details come later).

With this revolutionary method you waste no time getting right to the core of the key skill it takes to actually read. *Fast Phonics* achieves this by teaching only the 26 PHONETIC SOUND/ SYMBOLS first. The teaching of the alphabet NAMES and capital letters is postponed until a child is already reading three-letter words.

2

The "memory hook cartoons" are meticulously crafted to deliver the **STRONGEST POSSIBLE RECALL** of each visual symbol to its sound.

The cartoons are designed to be germane to the INSIDE of the letter itself, not crafted only as novel appendages hanging all over the OUTSIDE of the letter as in other phonics programs.

3

Fast Phonics continually requires small **choices of discrimination**, so the brain HAS to stay alert at all times while doing each lesson.

The course uses frequent fun checking/testing. The child himself knows at each stage what he retains and what he does not yet retain. This method **jettisons any possibility of having a lazy brain** while gaining all of the skills necessary to read.

4

Fast Phonics uses **both hemispheres of the brain** to log in all of the material:

The visual section: initially with the cartoons—later with the exercises.

The motor planning/tactile section: initially with the no-pencil tracing (using the pointer finger only) and hand motions, and later with having to manipulate the information within all of the other skills.

5

Vowels are taught with exceptional clarity.

Short vowels are treated as "one of the boys." They are learned right alongside ordinary consonants as if they were no different. When long vowels are introduced, their conversions from short to long are drilled (nailed) 160 times before those long vowels are ever used in a sentence. Once the child begins encountering them in sentences, he KNOWS how to decode them instantly.

6

Fast Phonics **builds HUMOR into the program** so that the student's emotions are happily enticed to dive into print with gusto!

Fast Phonics

the easy track to reading

Renée Ellison

Intensive, systematic, phonics instruction would heal the bulk of our nation's illiteracy problem. The whole-word, "look-say" approach has been responsible for its demise.

(Summarized from the works of Dr. Samuel Blumenfeld, author of *The New Illiterates*)

HOMESCHOOL
HOW-TO'S

Website: http://www.homeschoolhowtos.com
Email: info@homeschoolhowtos.com

Library of Congress Cataloging-in-Publication Data
Ellison, Renée R.
Fast phonics: the easy track to reading.
Durango, Colo.: Homeschool How-To's, c2017.
180 p.
Teach faster series.
Reading (Elementary).
Reading-- Phonetic method-- Handbooks, manuals, etc.
Language arts (Elementary).
Home schooling-- Curricula.
Education-- Parent participation.
Home schooling-- Curricula-- United States-- Handbooks, manuals, etc.
LC classification (Partial): LB1573 .E   2017
ISBN 978-0-9987894-0-8

Cover design by Erin Jones.
Printed in the United States of America
Book website: http://fastphonics.weebly.com/

Table of Contents

Introduction

Now you can teach your child to read, easily.

Want to experience the thrill of being the one to escort your child from the world of illiteracy to the world of literacy? Now you can do it, at home, in spare minutes—and you can do it without having to become a "phonics lawyer" to figure out how.

Your child is about to learn to read far faster than most children have ever learned to read before.

Why?

You will succeed in teaching your child to read quickly because you are your child's tutor and you will know exactly what to do. You are now going to be instantly trained (as you go) in the most direct, skillful reading techniques possible for tackling this job. You'll tutor with jaw-dropping efficiency—and your child will learn at record speed.

How?

With bull's-eye focus, this method cuts through the phonics jungle FOR YOU. It guides you through all the baby steps needed to give you amazing rapid-reading-results. All YOU do is hang on for the ride, turning pages. Yes, if you merely can turn pages, you can now teach your child to read.

Simple, clear instructions precede each small step, so that you never have to refer to a separate teacher's manual. These hold-your-hand directions are right in front of you, each step of the way. No preparations are needed.

These clear, "easy to grasp" instructions will penetrate your parenting brain, even if you feel you would be forever inferior to the task or are frequently prone to suffer from brain fog days.

All of this makes for an easier teaching job for the parent, but wait 'til you see how easy it is for the CHILD. If a basketball coach used the same method it would be like replacing the basketball hoop with a large bucket placed on the floor at the feet of a child and asking him to merely drop the ball in—while the coach says, "Way to go, buddy!"

The tightly designed memory hooks are so strong and the tactile-touch-imprinting is so engaging that the sound/symbols are retained almost as soon as they are met.

The student thoroughly conquers each step before proceeding onward, thus progressing incrementally from success to success. Complete mastery of each step is assured by frequent mini-testing, that doesn't FEEL like testing at all. It feels more like a "look-what-I-can-do" game.

This breakthrough new system initially eliminates all overwhelming reading obstacles (sources of confusion) while simultaneously stimulating excitement. Thus, even the student's emotions are happily enticed to dive into print with gusto.

Why was teaching reading NOT so easy before?

The past experimental method of sight-reading (also known as look-say) has been a dismal failure. It resulted in generations of readers who impulsively guessed at words rather than decoding them. This method relied on heavy repetition of a limited vocabulary by presenting full words to the child from the beginning, hoping that merely by seeing each word repeated OFTEN enough, the child would "learn" to read that way.

Think of the painstaking drill this necessitated, only to get the child's reading vocabulary up over a mere ten words. It resulted in two classic books being written about its consummate failure: one in 1955 called *Why Johnny Can't Read* and another in 1981, *Why Johnny Still Can't Read.*

Another experimental attempt at teaching reading was called the language experience approach. It, too, was tried and found to be another failure. It was supposed to work by having the child tell the teacher about something. The teacher took down the child's exact words in writing as he spoke them, with the expectation (a very faint hope) that the child could read the narrative later because he already knew the content. If he had any success even remembering the words at all, such a method limited the child's reading potential to his own narrow experience base—a very little world, indeed.

With such agonizingly demanding and arduous tasks, it is a wonder that teachers who tried these approaches remained in the profession. Both methods left children at sea when it came to decoding any new word.

Phonics to the rescue

Cracking the reading CODE is the only way to teach and to learn reading. This has been proven over and over throughout history.

Acquiring phonics skill is the only sure key to entering the kingdom of literacy, and **instantaneous sound/symbol recognition is the whole key-ring**. We have one key for this lock, and a different key for that lock. Decode-presto-open. Reading early and reading well is the reward.

Unfortunately, however, even with this time-tested optimal approach, most phonics programs throw far too much content at the child in the beginning. For starters, many of these programs don't ensure that the very first step is completely mastered—that of the sound/symbol connection. Instead, they barrage the child with over 80 symbols to "learn" simultaneously, with superficial results. These cumbersome approaches then proceed to "build" (i.e., throw additional reading tasks at the child way too soon) upon this shaky foundation. As a consequence, many a child winds up confused or labeled dyslexic.

Many of these current inefficient phonics programs require too much time, taking two full years (kindergarten and first grade) to complete—when, as you'll soon see, the whole process can be accomplished in far less time.

In addition, parents can find that they currently squander several hundred dollars on phonics programs that are saddled with needless trinkets and gimmicks, and then sadly find that their child still can't read fluently.

Keep in mind that you can teach a child to read using most any phonics program, but it may take you forever—or, at least, make you feel like it. Furthermore, most phonics programs are so tedious to teach for the average busy parent, it feels like you're being chained to teaching your child the Latin Vulgate. When taught too slowly, without making much headway, reading lessons can turn into a real chore and produce some serious student resistance, which the child may not be able to overcome for a long time.

Out with the old—in with the new

In this faster method, three traditional things are postponed.
Everything that could potentially confuse or overwhelm the child is

postponed. We want to get the child on the reading bus ASAP. The rest of the luggage is thrown in later. In the beginning we just want to get some exciting success happening soon.

One:
CAPITAL LETTERS are postponed

Initially, the capital letters can wait. In this program they are not taught along with the lowercase letters. The child is taught to recognize only ONE symbol per sound, using only the lowercase symbols.

Two:
The ALPHABET is postponed

Yes, learning the alphabet <u>names</u>, too, can wait. To begin with, only the PHONETIC SOUND—the sound we use to actually read— is taught.

We don't teach the alphabet song. (If the child knows it already, just ignore that for now.) The letter "b" is not taught to the child as the letter "bee" at all. We omit the alphabet letter NAMES that are taught in that song, entirely. The "b" is only taught as the phonetic SOUND "buh" from the beginning—and it stays that way until that one sound becomes an automatic correct verbal response every time the symbol is seen.

By eliminating these and other sources of confusion, we immediately reduce the reading decoding challenge from having to learn over 80 new symbol/sound connections to only 26.

So, to review, in the beginning, we teach ONLY the phonetic sound using ONLY the lowercase letter. This builds a strong, unshakeable decoding confidence in the child. With such a rock solid foundation the rest of the reading skill is acquired with remarkable ease.

Three:
ALLITERATION, as a primary decoding tool, is postponed

Using alliteration as a primary tool for helping children remember the sound/symbol connection—as some phonics programs do—is a waste of time. These programs rely heavily on the auditory (hearing) input of the sound to anchor the word. They use catchy sentences like "Busy bees buzz by blueberries" or "Allie the alligator adored apples all afternoon."

Alliteration won't teach SYMBOL recognition. Give the child the VISUAL CONNECTION and the powerful "seeing recognition skill" begins to develop. Some alliteration can then be used afterwards for fun, but not under the delusion that we are providing a VISUAL tool to unlock the SYMBOL. The touch and the vision have a long way to go to catch up with the hearing—which has been fully operational, working at mach speed, since birth, five or six years ahead of the other. Now, our job is to concentrate with bull's-eye focus on the heretofore unknown part of reading: the contribution of the hands and the eyes to the decoding process.

In this faster method, three new things are ADDED.

One:
Cartoons

We tuck the visual key to unlocking each letter into the letter shape. The key sits subliminally IN the letter. The cartoon picture of the letter leads the child directly to the sound. He gets there in a heartbeat and happily finds that he can recall that same image each time thereafter. We hide the key in plain sight. In addition, the cartoons succeed in waking up happy emotions for the student to bring to the task of decoding. Well aimed, tight cartoons trigger the brain to make concrete instant associations with the sound, each and every time the letter is encountered.

Next we anchor the cartoon with a consistent, single trigger word and an isolated sound. The same word is said by the parent/teacher each and every time the child sees the symbol. For example, mountain is always used for "m". Further words like mess, mush, mud, monkeys, motorcycles and muscles, are not added, too. The child will make those additional connections later. Right now he needs a single, secure way to remember each phonetic sound—not multiple ways. Initially, the key needs to fit into the lock the same way EVERY TIME.

Two:
Tracing

We further reinforce the sound/symbol retention with large, exact tracing using the smooth clicker end of a pen (not using a pencil, which is later used for actual printing). Accurate tracing is the objective for every day, until the symbol is mastered via the touch (as well as the sound and sight). We begin by having the child trace the letters in the direction of the arrows, on unusually large letters. Thus, from the start, the child learns to know the letter in his fingers, tactily.

Because the tracing step doesn't need the finer motor skill necessary to actually print with a pencil, a much younger child can be taught to read, ahead of that other slower brain development. This additionally means that any child (including students with dyslexia) can be taught to read, by now using the cartoons and the tracing where both the hand and eye work simultaneously to cement the sound/symbol connection without error. With this lavish amount of multi-sensory focused imprinting, decoding victories are won rapidly.

Three:
Testing

Plain-letter testing charts are included to provide frequent mini-testing. The child constantly goes back and forth between the charts with the teaching aids (of cartoons and the tracing arrows) to the charts with no teaching aids to see what he retains. Nothing gets lost in the cracks—because there are no cracks. Via these charts, the child knows at ALL TIMES exactly what he has retained and what he hasn't.

The overall aim of your teaching in this program is mastery.

Throughout the entire course, mastery of each step is the goal. **Teaching a child to read is an exact science that is every bit as sequential as teaching math.** If one step is not learned for MASTERY, the later steps built upon it cause the entire reading edifice to wobble and in many cases completely crash.

If the child is in any way iffy with any step, you can up the praise and slow down. If a child needs it, going slowly and thoroughly through all the reading steps is the precise route to faster progress in the long run. For such a child, slow IS fast. Each step must be secure. When you can't go forward, go wide. Enrich and review and practice some more on the step you are currently on. Aim to eliminate any decoding hesitation on each level, as you go.

No matter what the phonics program is that you're using, **the child can falter if you don't drill each mini-skill until it is automatic.** Reading failure is serious stuff. Reading failure eventually morphs into self-esteem problems, which can then morph into socialization traumas. Trouble with reading can ruin a life. It is very important to take the time to teach phonics well. Teach with patience, using consistent academic discipline. Olympic coaches hover over beginnings, for good reason. They have their eye ever on the future.

Do not leap ahead, enticing the child to put letters together pre-maturely to read, until that is the actual next step. Don't assume he knows each step. Instead, test it, as the course indicates all along the way, to be sure.

Conclusion:

This course has been meticulously groomed in every detail for your success. It provides the utmost in phonetic CLARITY and phonetic SIMPLICITY.

Each step has been carefully crafted to powerfully, lastingly imprint the brain the first time each skill is met. It is loaded with additional subtle strategic memory hooks throughout, each of which contributes to lasting retention.

This imprinting continues subliminally for hours afterwards, even when the student is doing something else entirely. This incubation process creates sure advances that are often seen immediately in the next teaching session.

In the first step, the right brain, through well-aimed, precisely targeted pictures and no pencil tracing, entices the left brain to do more than it ever thought possible, and to do it easier. And that's just the beginning.

Next steps:

After these first vital steps are conquered, the child reads two-letter words and then swiftly transitions to three-letter words that are packaged inside a host of silly sentences and funny stories.

Additional phonics steps follow, which deliver the same amazingly fast and effective results. These further steps are explained as you work through the book.

The big picture:

> Reading widens life. We're all greedy for life, you know, but our short span of existence can't give us all that we hunger for. Our time is too short and our capacity not large enough. But in books we get to experience far more of life, vicariously.
> (Elizabeth Goudge, *A City of Bells*)

Because reading unlocks more of the big, wide world to all of us, we must unlock the door to reading for our children. We can do this by teaching them phonics in the easiest and swiftest manner possible.

When we teach a child to read (using phonics) we're actually putting hooks into the abstract by capturing sounds and turning them into symbols. We drag the auditory (the language that has been stored in the ear/hearing) into the visual field of the child. He will now SEE what he has been hearing for years. And in this particular program, his hand, via tracing, will reinforce the specific details of what he sees. Turn the page and you can begin this exciting adventure today.

Please note:

Due to the limitations of the English language regarding pronoun usage, it is bunglesome to repeatedly refer to "the student" as "he/she" every time. Therefore, for the purposes of this text, the generic "he" will be used to connote both genders, throughout these materials, with no slight intended.

1955: <u>Why Johnny Can't Read</u>

This book by Rudolf Flesch, published decades after US schools adopted the "look-say" method and/or the "language-experience" approach, revealed that the use of those programs had drastically lowered literacy scores.

1981: <u>Why Johnny Still Can't Read</u>

This follow-up book (again, written by Flesch) spurred another man, Dr. Samuel Blumenfeld (the then editor of the Universal Library at Grosset and Dunlap), to further address the problem of growing illiteracy in the US. Blumenfeld's earlier research had resulted in his eye-opening book, *The New Illiterates*, in 1973. In 1983 Dr. Blumenfeld published the first of 14 editions of *Alpha-Phonics*—a brilliant, succinct restoration of the basic principles of phonics. This pointed the way out of the prevailing reading wilderness.

2000: Johnny *can* read

By the start of this century some private and public schools had begun to return to phonics, led by an aggressive home school movement whose pioneers insisted upon teaching phonetic decoding skills—the method successfully used by the Puritans, with the result that the literacy rate in the New England colonies was about 90% at the end of the 18th century. The problem remains, however, that phonics programs require too much time, and have not been simplified *enough*. But happily, now all that has changed. Today there is a far easier way to teach children to read.

2017: Now Johnny can learn to read EASILY

Building on the growing recognition of the superiority of phonics programs over look-say programs as the best way to learn how to read, we now have an easier and faster road to get there. With *Fast Phonics*, a child can learn to read with remarkably strong retention and accuracy—and can now get there with record-breaking speed. Years of phonics instruction can be reduced to months using this radically advanced approach. Bull's-eye memory hooks get the job done with far less effort. Taught this way, children not only learn to read quickly, but enjoy the process of getting there, too.

Phonics at a glance
(a simple overview):

1. Phonetic sounds
(short vowels automatically included)

2. Simple 3-letter words

3. Long vowels

4. Basic sight words

5. Blends (ch, sp, etc.)

6. Diphthongs:

2 vowels together
that make a new sound
(e.g. "oy" in boy)

Using these 3 charts to teach each group of six letters gives a child a...

Triple imprint
to sound/symbol mastery

1

The Cartoon Chart

...introduces each letter with a strong, visual memory hook...tucking the clue to the SOUND into the SHAPE itself...hiding the "key" in plain sight.

2

The Tester Chart

...provides a means to instantly and repeatedly check retention, both from the cartoon memory hooks chart and the tracing skills chart. The brain is never allowed to be lazy. It is constantly asked to make choices in little discriminations.

3

The Tracer Chart

...cements the details of six letters at a time into the brain via the additional sense of touch. This chart exposes the child to the awareness of all of the chart's letters at once, equally, AND then teaches him how to trace those letters accurately. It is used, at first, as a speedy drive-through overview, with the parent guiding the child's hand, and secondly, is used again, more slowly, as a means to teach the child how to trace the letters himself. This chart is employed with the belief that if the child can't eventually draw each symbol shape accurately FROM MEMORY, he doesn't know the letter well enough.

~~~~~~~~~~~~

How to use the Cartoon Chart

This chart shows cartoons drawn around the letters. Use this fun chart to further teach each of the letters in detail. Share the short catchy cartoon story that matches each letter, and finish teaching the letter by reinforcing it further with each letter's playful, attendant hand motion. Both the short cartoon story and the hand motions are found on the pages just before each cartoon chart.

When finished with the teaching of the six cartooned letters, test the letters RANDOMLY on this same cartoon chart by asking: "Which one says dog-duh?" [for example]. Then eventually re-test on the plain letters testing chart. If the child can't remember, point to it FOR him, initially, and then re-teach whatever letters are still not mastered.

Eliminating "b" and "d" confusion:

To help the child avoid confusion between the "b" and "d", have him make two fists. Have him hold his fists knuckle to knuckle in front of his chest and then lift both thumbs straight up out of the fist. Note the "b" shape made by the left fist when the thumb is sticking up. Tell him, "First came the stick, and then the ball." Then draw his attention to the "d" shape made by the right fist, where the stick comes AFTER the ball. Finally, teach him to say: "The baby walked the dog." The baby always comes first.

~~~~~~~~~~~~

How to use the Tester Chart
(the plain letters)

This chart has no cartoons and no dots and arrows. In other words, it has no memory aids. The goal with this chart is to constantly test the child by going back and forth between the charts WITH the memory hooks to this chart with NO memory hooks.

One
To test, first ask: "Which letter says __?" and CALL OUT the phonetic sounds (buh, duh, kuh, zuh, etc.) on that chart in random order.

Two
Next, test by POINTING to random letters and have the child COME UP with the sound himself.

Three
Have the child TRACE each letter accurately from memory by himself. Does he know the starting dot/point? And does he trace the letter in the correct directions?

Re-teach any letter still not known by going back to the charts with teaching aids. Do not move on to new letters/charts until the child has mastered the current ones.

~~~~~~~~~~~~

How to use the Tracer Chart
(the chart with the starting dots and directional arrows)

First use: Speedy drive-through overview

At the beginning, you do this chart TOGETHER. Have the child begin at the starting dot to trace the letter with you, with the smooth clicker end of a pen (no writing with a pencil at this point).

Guide the child's hand (which grips the smooth-ended pen in his fist) by cupping his hand in yours and tracing/moving through all the letters at a steady, smooth pace. You, as the parent/teacher, are doing most of the moving effort, essentially driving the child through the symbols, while he hangs on for the ride. Say the trigger word and its isolated beginning sound as you trace each letter TOGETHER. Have the child echo you, as you go, verbally saying each letter's trigger word and its isolated sound immediately after you.

If the child is very small, he will be sitting on your lap as you do this. If the child is older, pull your chair up behind him and reach around him to cup his hand initially, until he gets the hang of it.

The goal of this exercise is merely EXPOSURE and rapid tactile imprinting—not mastery.

Second use of the Tracer Chart:

Now, use this same chart again to teach the child how to actually master the tracing, himself. Tell the child that this step is called **tap and trace**.

After you have introduced the cartoon chart, come back to this dot and arrow chart and do the speedy drive-through of this tracer chart once more. Then, in this same session, continue to use this chart, by going through it a second time, now far slower, for TRAINING the actual tracing.

The goal this time through is to have the child master tracing the letters accurately by himself. Do BOTH the speedy drive-through and the slower tracing instruction for EACH teaching session until all six letters on this chart, and the cartoon chart, are mastered, before proceeding with the next chart of six new letters. Space your teaching/ learning/ review sessions apart throughout the day—at least twice a day (and more, if and when the child seems eager).

In this second step, get the child to trace the letter accurately any way you can. You can even discard using the smooth clicker end of the pen and have the child just use his pointer finger, if that is easier. You, as the parent, can lead the way through the tracing stroke by staying slightly ahead of him, pointing the way using a colored straw, a chopstick or a pen's smooth clicker end. The main thing is that you want to keep your hand OUT of the visual field so the child can see the roadway ahead of him—so he can actually SEE the starting dot and the direction of the arrows. Remember to continually say the trigger word and its isolated sound for him, having him echo you verbally as he proceeds through the chart.

Teach the child to TAP the starting point of each of the six letters, FIRST, and then test just this beginning skill before completing the tracing. Can he find the starting place on each letter on the plain-letters-chart? When he CAN, then go back and begin to actually teach the full tracing of the letters.

TRACE the letter, following the arrows. Continue this practice until he can tap and trace the letters without the arrows on the plain letter's tester chart. Check his retention by frequently referring back to that tester chart.

Note: When following the tracing arrows, do not lift your pen from the paper while tracing/printing the letters. This means you'll be tracing up AND down on some of the letter's lines. This makes the child's handwriting motions more fluid, and ultimately increases speed.

Exceptions are f, k, t, x, and y —each of which requires two or three separately-made strokes.

~~~~~~~~~~~~

Optional: **Phonics Song**

If you are musically inclined and want to teach a phonics song, just substitute phonetic sounds for the alphabet names in the traditional alphabet song. That is all there is to it. As you sing it SLOWLY for and with your child, point to the letters arranged below to match the melody line and rhythm. (Use a pointer like a pencil or a chopstick to keep your hand out of the student's visual field.)

Be sure that you are using the correct phonetic pronunciation for each phonetic sound. If you are not sure of the sound, look at the beginning sound of each of the trigger words used for teaching the cartoons in this course. If you think of the word "abacus" (the tool used for counting in math), it will ensure that you say the first three sounds accurately. Practice the entire song many times privately, to get it right, before attempting to teach it to your child.

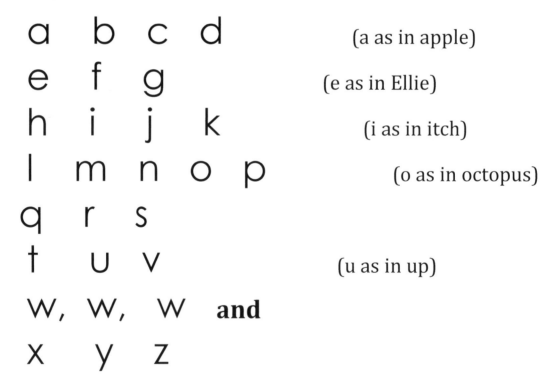

a	b	c	d	(a as in apple)
e	f	g		(e as in Ellie)
h	i	j	k	(i as in itch)
l	m	n	o	p	(o as in octopus)
q	r	s		
t	u	v		(u as in up)
w, w, w	**and**			
x	y	z		

End the song with,

> **"Phonics sounds, hey can't you see,**
> **will help me read quite rapidly."**

Optional: **Lowercase Foam Puzzle**

Directions:

Lowercase foam puzzles can be purchased from at least these two sources: Lauri's at Amazon.com and a more generic one from a Dollar Tree retail store. Lay the puzzle on a cookie tray for a stable surface.

Have child match six foam letters with only the six letters on the one chart you are currently teaching. Pull those few appropriate foam letters out of the puzzle ahead of time. Have the child place the foam letters on TOP of the chart letters that they match. This exercise causes the child to both "feel" the letter and to begin visual discrimination (via seeing each letter as different from the other letters) on that page.

Next have the child re-insert the six foam letters into the puzzle. It should be easy because there are only six spaces blank on the puzzle at a time. If the child doesn't SEE a vacant shape location in the puzzle frame right away, you can help him. Gradually withdraw your help in subsequent sessions.

Fish for letters

Another fun way to use the foam puzzle is to have the child go fishing for the letters in water. Fill a shallow plastic storage container with water. Hand the child a large slatted serving spoon to fish the letters out with. Lay each piece on a dry washrag to absorb any remaining moisture. Say the sound and then re-insert the letter into the puzzle frame.

Learning letters

a - f

- **cartoon chart** (includes catchy cartoon stories and hand motion theater)

- **tester chart**

- **tracer chart**

Note the accurate phonetic sound of this letter,

f: rest the top teeth on the bottom lip, and force air through the teeth

Cartoon stories and hand motions for letter introductions

When teaching the cartoons, be sure to use the "phonetic sound," which is the same sound that begins each trigger word

Sometimes a little bit of "**hand motion theater**" can mean the difference between a child loving a letter instantly vs. leaving it out there somewhere in a dull gray fog.

Note: In teaching the letter hand movements below, do not refer to the terms "right" and "left." Instead, anchor those directions (draw the child's attention) to an object, a window or a door location on the right or left wall of the room, and have him move his arm in *that* direction.

apple "a"
Alice adores apples. Apples hang on trees.

Make a "c" by cupping the left hand into a "c" shape for the profile of an apple. Apply the pointer finger of the right hand to the right edge of the apple to make a tree trunk. Then bring the apple forward to take a bite out of its side nearest you.

baby "b"
Baby buggies bounce. [or strollers ☺]

Fist up the left hand with the thumb up, and bounce (hop) the baby buggy on the table—three hops—traveling the fist in front of the child's body from left to right.

cat "c"
Cats climb cleverly.

The left hand creates a "c" shape on the table. Hold that shape in the hand rigidly while leaping it in the direction of the ceiling, high overhead.

dog "d"

Dogs despise doors.

Place the open palm of your right hand on the front of your face. Pretend to be the dog, pushing against the palm.

elephant "e"

Ellie the elephant munches on excellent eggs.

Swing the right arm forward (for the elephant's trunk), grab an imaginary egg, and swing his trunk (your arm) back into the mouth.

"f" fix

Fred fixes frames and furniture.

The left elbow is on the table with that arm straight up (ceiling direction). Drop the hand at the wrist to look like a hammer head. Tap that elbow three times on the table as if it were pounding with a hammer, and then saw sideways midway on that left forearm, using the right hand's pointer finger.

cat

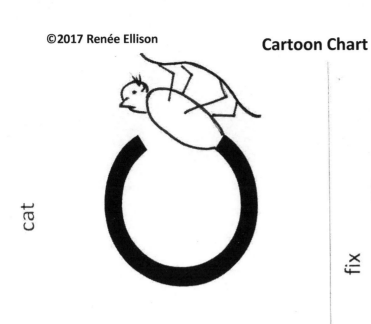

fix

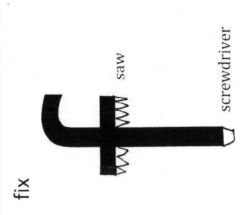

saw

screwdriver

baby

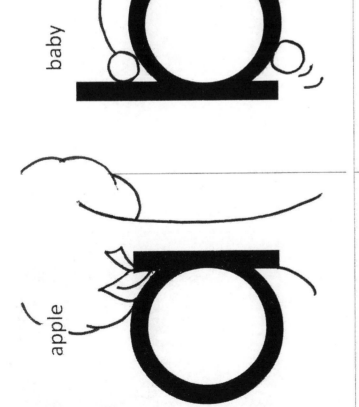

elephant

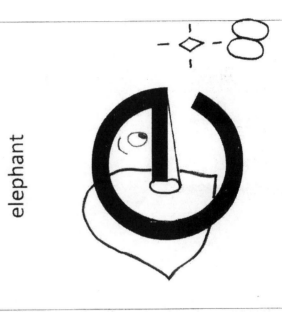

apple

dog

cat

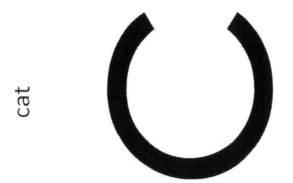

fix

baby

elephant

apple

dog

cat

fix

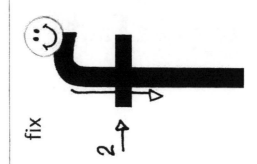

baby

elephant

apple

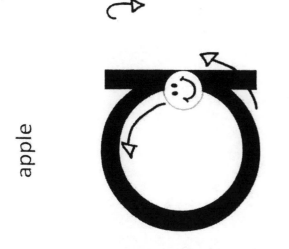

dog

Eliminate "b" and "d" confusion

**Make a fist with both hands.
Stick the thumbs up.**

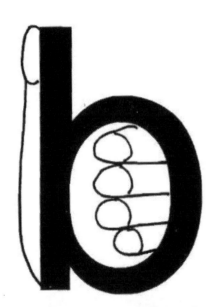 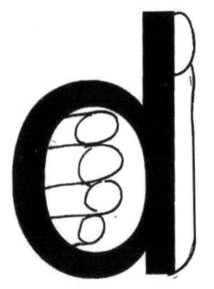

The baby walks the dog!

b = stick before circle

d = circle followed by stick

Eliminating "b" and "d" confusion

Have the student travel along the line with his pointer finger.

When he bumps into a letter, ask him, "Is this the handle of the buggy [buh] or is it a doggie-face [duh]?"

Cover up lines you aren't reading with blank paper.

b...d...b...d...d

b...d...b...d...b

b...b...d...b...d

d...b...d...d...b

d...b...d...b...d

Learning letters

g - l

- **cartoon chart** (includes catchy cartoon stories and hand motion theater)

- **tester chart**

- **tracer chart**

Note the accurate phonetic sounds of these 2 letters:

h :   puff of air in the back of the throat

l :   say "ul" with the tongue pressing the front of the roof of the mouth

Cartoon stories and hand motions
for letter introductions

"g" give

Gladys gives good gifts.

The student traces the letter shape as the teacher says

**"Gladys went all around town to get a
gift to go down to give Mr. Grumpy."**

"h" hat

Heidi hides under her hat.

Start with the arms holding an imaginary hat high overhead,
and then lower an imaginary hat to the head and slide it to the
left of the head.

"i" itch

Icky mosquito bites itch.

Itch the inside of the left forearm with right hand fingers in a
straight line, then press a dot above the itch line to indicate exactly where the mosquito bit...(making the dot above the "i").

When you get a mosquito bite, you want to **itch it!**

29

"j" jam

Jam the jelly in the jar.

"Jerry jammed the jelly in the jar and then joyously jerked it out again." Act like you are scooping the jam back out of the jar with a "j" stroke.

"k" kite

Kites crash.

Fully extend the left arm up as a straight tree, then take the right fist and smash it into the middle of the tree while yelling out, "crash IN!" and "fall OUT! [for making the lower part of the lowercase "k"]. End with the right fist on the right side of the child's body, towards the floor, as if the kite fell to the ground.

"l" ladder

Larry likes "ladder landings!"

Make a "ladder landing." Extend the right arm straight up into the air, finger tips pointed to the ceiling. Using the palm of the right hand, draw a straight line through the air down from the imaginary top of a ladder to crash onto the table, while yelling out "ladder landing!"

Cartoon Chart

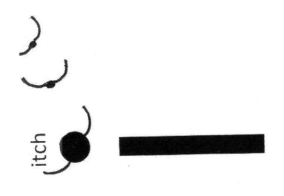

itch

ladder

hat

kite

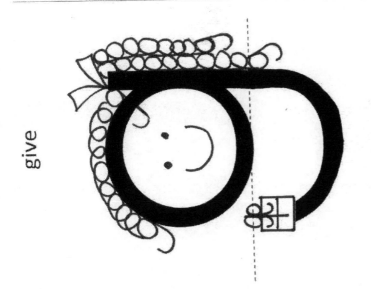

give

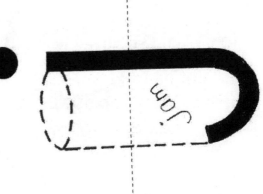

jam

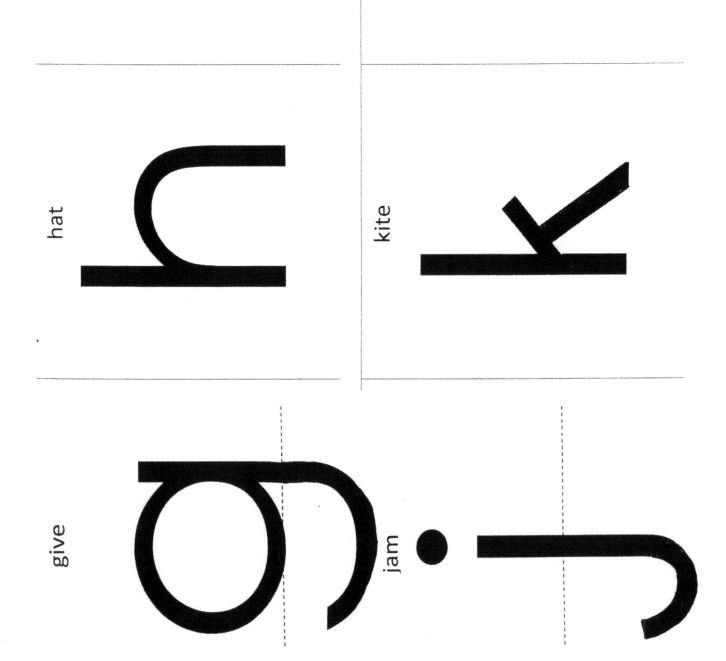

Fast Phonics

Tracer Chart

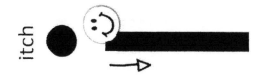

itch

ladder

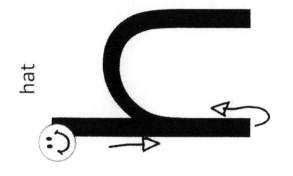

hat

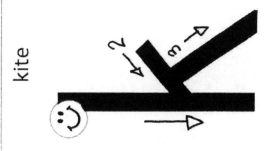

kite

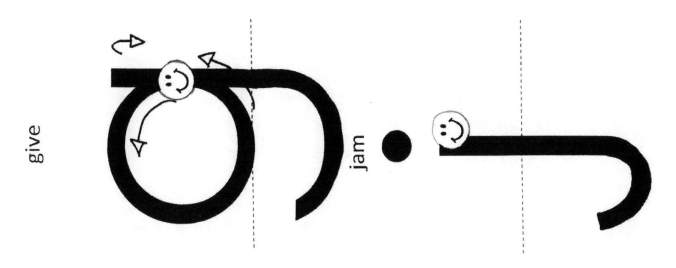

give

jam

Learning letters

- **cartoon chart** (includes catchy cartoon stories and hand motion theater)

- **tester chart**

- **tracer chart**

Note the accurate phonetic sounds of these 3 letters:

m: press lips tightly together, and make the sound in the back of the throat

n: with the tongue pressed to the roof of the mouth, push air through the nasal cavity

r: say "er" or "roar"

Cartoon stories and hand motions
for letter introductions

"m" mountain

Mom motorcycles through the mountains in the moonlight.

Trace over this letter shape while telling this story. Mom goes DOWNtown to rent the motorcycle, and then returns to her starting place (trace back up the stick part of the letter) and then makes two humps, as if she is motoring through the mountains.

"n" nose

Ned's nose is NOT small.

The student strokes his own nose (using his right hand)in the following pattern. Begin at the top of his nose, stroke the left side, and then trace that side back up; go across the bridge of the nose and come down the right side while saying "nice nose!"

"o" octopus

The odd octopus ogles oxygen.

Clasp both arms overhead to make an "o."

"p" Pa

"Pa, the porcupine is about to poke you!"

While tracing this letter, explain to the child that on his first downward stoke he is pretending that he is pulling on papa's pant leg to get his attention. After that, the student traces back up the stick to go back up to pa's face, then circles the face to get his full attention to point out that the porcupine is just about to poke pa in the leg.

"q" queen

The queen asks too many questions!

Drape a long robe/towel down the back of the child. Have him grasp it over his shoulders and then proceed to walk very slowly and stately, saying "walk like a queeeeeen" while dragging the towel's "tail" on the ground out behind him. Then, point out the tail on the actual letter.

"r" ran

Rita ran the race and the crowd roared.

Trace the letter while you tell this little story. Rita ran a race. Shortly after the beginning of the race there was a split in the road; the race had a turn off road to Rita's left (but OUR right, looking at the "r" from our direction). She MISSED the turn off and ran straight to the bottom of the road, but the crowd was located at the end of the race at the end of the turn off road, so she had to run doubly fast back up the road to the beginning and take the turn off to get to the end where the crowd was. She ran so fast, she still won the race!

Cartoon Chart

octopus

ran

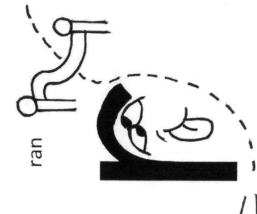

nose

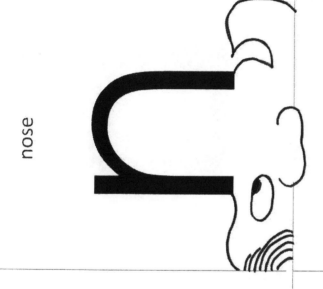

queen

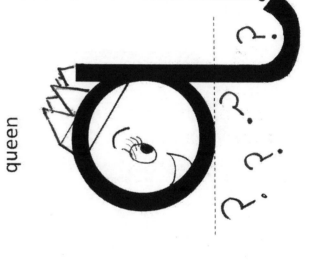

mountain

pa

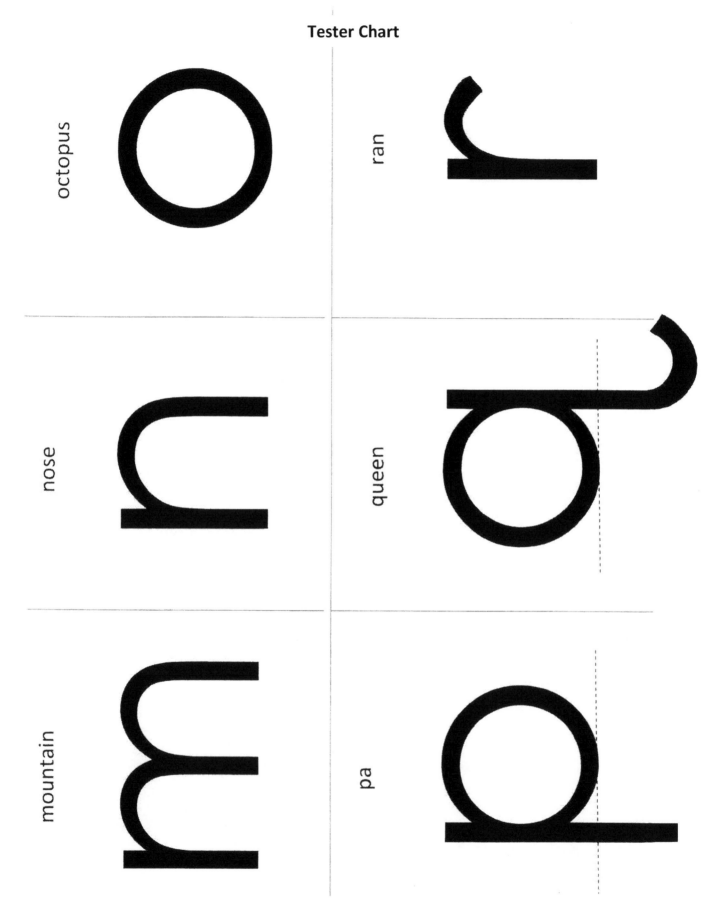

octopus

ran

nose

queen

mountain

pa

Tracer Chart

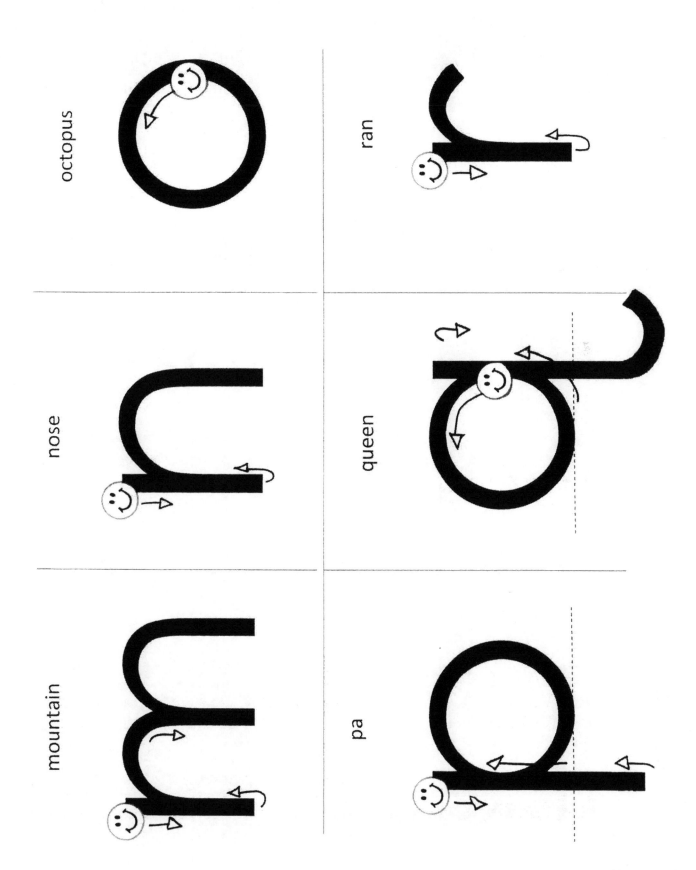

octopus

nose

mountain

ran

queen

pa

Eliminating "p" and "q" confusion

Have the student travel along the line with his pointer finger.

When he bumps into a letter, ask him, "Did you bump into papa's leg?" [puh] "or did you bump into the queen's face?" [quah]

Use a blank paper to cover up lines you aren't reading.

q...p...p...p...q

..q...p...q...q...

p...q...p...p p

q...p...p...q...q

p...q...q...p...q

q...q...p...p...q

Eliminating "b", "d", "p", "q" confusion

First have the student tell you, "Does the tail go up or down?"

If it is up, ask him, "Did you run into a bar of a buggy or a dog's face?"

If it is down, ask, "Did you run into pa's leg or a queen's face?"

Note: In all beginning reading, not just on this page, but with actual three-letter words, have the child track with his pointer finger under EVERY letter in EACH and EVERY word. Otherwise, he is prone to lose his one-to-one correspondence, and his reading fluency suffer.

d...q...p...d...p

b...d...q...b...q

q...b...p...d... *[repeat]*

Learning letters

S - Z

- **cartoon chart** (includes catchy cartoon stories and hand motion theater)

- **tester chart**

- **tracer chart**

Note the accurate phonetic sound of the letter **X**:

➢ Use the ending sound of ax, box, fox

➢ Do **not** initially use the words xylophone, x-ray or exit

Cartoon stories and hand motions for letter introductions

"s" snake

Sam the snake slithers and smiles.

Trace the "s" while saying the phrase above.

"t" Tom

Tom talks tons.

When he gets REALLY excited, Tom flings his arms out to his sides to express himself even more! Fling your arms out to the sides, horizontally.

"u" up

Uppity up!

Hold both arms up, helplessly, like a little baby saying "up, up, please." Then switch roles to pretend to be the parent. Using both arms, scoop down and come UP "u"-nder an imaginary baby to lift him up—saying to the baby "uppity up we go."

"v" valley

Victory in the valley! No vipers!

Vic saw no vipers as he walked through the very vertical valley!

Create a "v" for "valley" with forearms pointing in the direction of the ceiling corners and elbows together, and then drop your head forward through the arms (valley) as if passing through it. Then hold up a V (made with the right hand's pointer and tall man fingers extended while holding the pinkie under with the thumb, to form a V) for victory, like Winston Churchill frequently showed with *his* two fingers to encourage the British Empire not to give up during World War II.

"w" water

Water wanders.

Flop the right hand on the table back and forth in a "w" shape.

"x" ax

The ax attacks trees.

The student crosses his mid-forearms and flings both arms down to each side of his body, as if axing two trees simultaneously in both directions.

"y" yo-yo

Yes! on yo-yos!

Use the sign-language for "yes": fist the right hand with the thumb up, and then extend the baby finger—that's the sign.

Then switch the image to the yo-yo. Pretend to let an imaginary yo-yo run from the student's high left of his body to his waist, swiping the air with his left hand.

Next, pretend that the yo-yo drops off that finger and disappears. The student then starts a second yo-yo, with his right hand swiping the air in the opposite direction (from high right to low left diagonally in front of his body).

"z" zebra

Zebras walk in zigzags.

The student rubs his torso from side to side to make zebra stripes running sideways. Begin on the left side of the body, making a "z" shape.

up

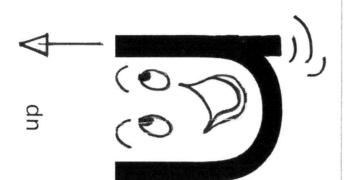

zebra

yes! yo-yo's!

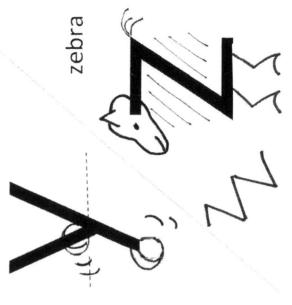

Tom talks

ax

water

snake

valley

up

Tom talks

snake

yes! yo-yo's!

zebra

water

ax

valley

up

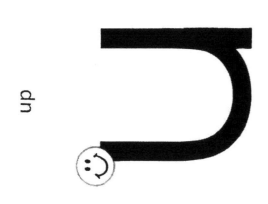

zebra

yes! yo-yo's!

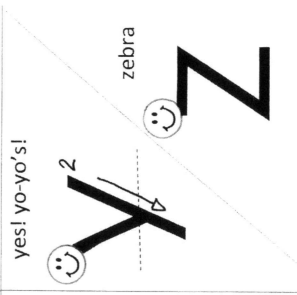

Tom talks

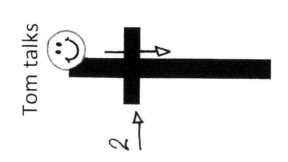

water

ax

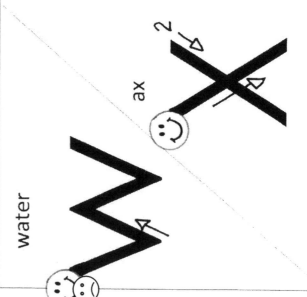

snake

valley

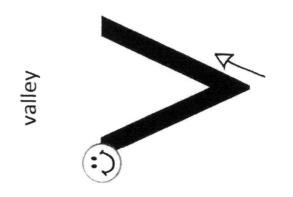

Final letter testing, using flashcards

Once your student has mastered all of the letters using the charts, further test all 26 letters, all scrambled up together. To do this, make the following pages into flashcards. Photocopy pages 50-54. Be sure to photocopy these pages on one side only—only SINGLE-sided—because you'll want to be able to see all of the letters at once, sometimes, and you can't do that if half of the letters are on the backsides of the cards. Then cut them out and tape each one to one side of a 3x5 index card.

Begin to drill the cards, laying out six random cards on the table at a time. (Use only three cards if you're dealing with a child younger than five years of age.) The child picks up the card that you call out at random. (Be sure to use its phonetic sound and trigger word.) Note carefully which cards cause him to hesitate. After he hands you his retrieved stack of six, quietly pull out the more troubling cards and mix them in with your remaining larger stack of cards to be set out again with a different batch of six.

Continue to drill in this way, until the student rapidly picks up all of the cards correctly with no hesitation.

Now change the game. Re-test yet one final time. This time, have the child both say the letter sounds aloud himself and pick up the cards in any order he desires. You, as the teacher, say nothing in this go-round. Do this drill as many times as needed—until all of the cards/ sounds are mastered, with the student being able to initiate the phonetic sound himself.

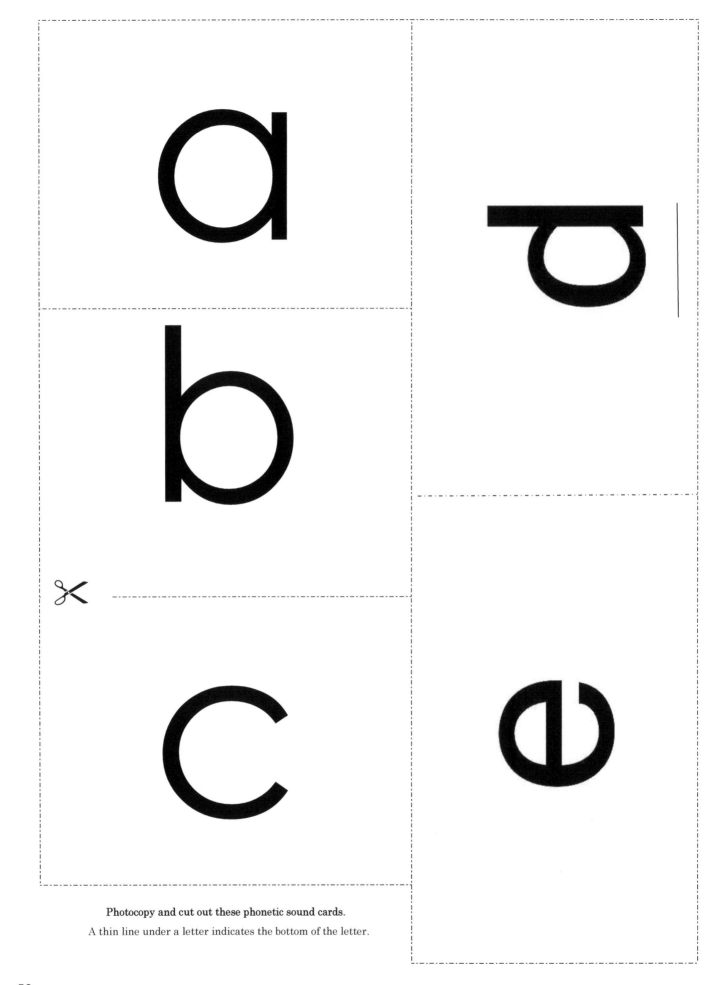

Photocopy and cut out these phonetic sound cards.

A thin line under a letter indicates the bottom of the letter.

50

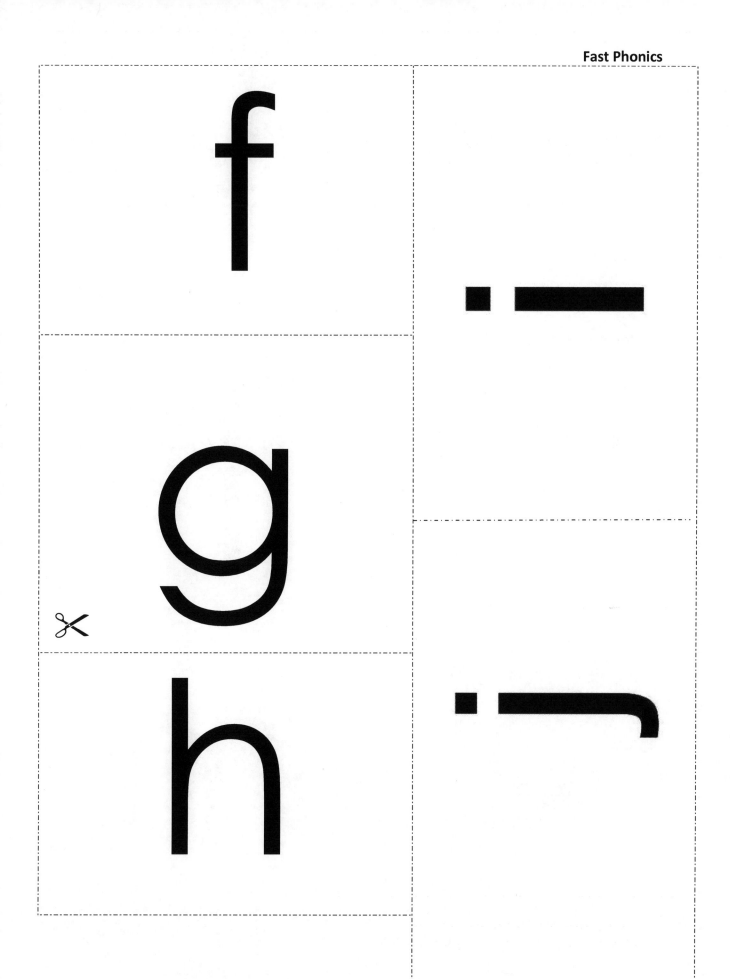

f

i

g

h

j

n

k

l

o

m

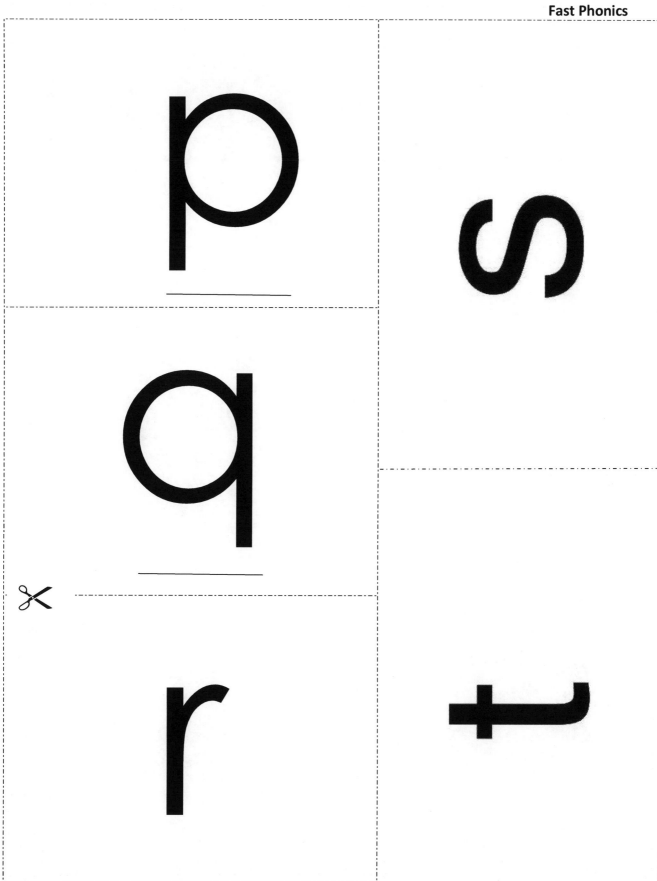

p

q

s

r

t

x

y

U

V

W

54

Final tester flashcard of the ⟶ **single lowercase letters**

Photocopy this one letter and cut it out to tape to a 3x5 card.

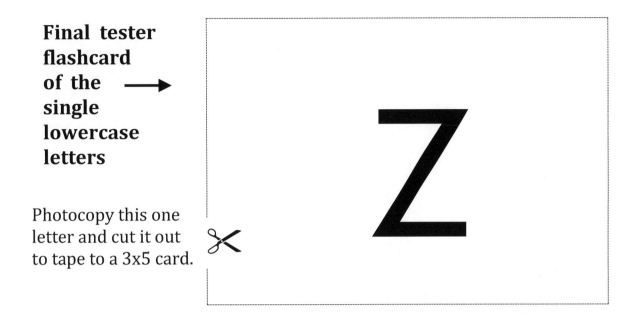

3-letter test

On the following page's three-letter test, have the child point to or circle the correct letter in each row. Place a half sheet of blank paper under each row to help the student track down the page without getting lost. (Make a photocopy of page 56 if you want to retain a master copy to use later with another child.)

Test down the left column of letters first and then test the right column at another point later in the day, or on the following day, as a second test. Call out any letter (within the three letters presented) to see if the child identifies and circles the one you said. If the child gets the majority of them correct, in both tests, then move on to the next page/step. If not, then go back and review the previous steps.

Note: The pictures down the center of the page are used to identity each row, instead of using numbers. The pictures have nothing to do with the sounds within that row. Their sole purpose is to replace numbering the rows.

Student Phonics Sounds Test #1
Circle whichever one of the three you hear the teacher say.

a c e		a c e
b f d		b f d
g j q		g j q
h l k		h l k
i p r		i p r
m o n		m o n
s x z		s x z
v u w		v u w
t y q		t y q
d f b		d f b
q j g		q j g
w u v		w u v
n o m		n o m

56

Introduce first words

This is an exciting "aha" step, showing the child the reward of all the hard work he has been doing, learning phonetic sounds/ letters.

This list contains 15 simple two-letter words. Show the child how you "read" them by sliding your finger slowly through the dots from the first letter to the second letter while you simultaneously keep the sound going until you run into the second letter.

At first, you, as the parent/teacher slowly read the letters and words aloud, having the child watch the process and echo you. But then go through the list a second time, helping the child do the decoding task himself. Be sure to liberally praise all of his beginning efforts in this direction, as you guide him. It may take several times through to get the hang of it. The teacher, alone, says the small print phrase, each time, at the end of each word. This begins to enlist the student's comprehension.

Make flashcards of the two-letter-word pages that follow several pages later. Photocopy these pages, cut them apart and tape them to the front of 3x5 cards.

First words

i.....f ⟶ if   (if it rains)

i.....t ⟶ it   (it is daytime)

i.....s ⟶ is   (is it night-time?)

i.....n ⟶ in   (in the box)

o.....n ⟶ on   (on the table)

o.....x ⟶ ox   (an ox is big)

a.....t ⟶ at   (at the edge)

a.....x ⟶ ax   (an ax cuts trees)

a.....m ⟶ am   (I am me!)

a.....n ⟶ an   (an alligator)

a.....s ⟶ as   (as I eat, I get full)

u.....p ⟶ up   (up the valley)

a.....d ⟶ ad   (here is the ad)

u.....s ⟶ us   (we are us!)

e.....x ⟶ ex   (the letter x)

in

on

if

it

is

am

ox

an

at

ax

as

up

ad

ex

us

First story (2-letter words)

Now the two-letter words are put into the child's first fun reading story. There are no capital letters, because the child has not learned those yet. Slide a blank 3x5 card under each line as the child begins to read it himself, to help him keep his place. You read the entire thing to him first—with lots of expression, emphasizing the words that are in bold font. Once your student has mastered reading the story WORDS himself, proceed to then teach him to use EXPRESSION by noting the punctuation. (*Note:* we know that the use of the word "am" in this story is poor grammar, but it makes for fun beginning reading.)

is it an ox ?

it **is** an ox.

if it **is**...?

it **is**!

tis an ox.

na, tis an ax.

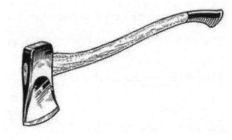

an ox it am.

if it **am** an ox, **it is** !

na, an ax it am.

if it **am** an ax, it **is** !

an ax is on an ox.

an ax is **in** an ox, it **is** !   ug !

an ex is **on** an ox.

up, ox, up !

ox, up, up !

an **ox** + an **ax** + an **ex** am
   in an in [inn].

it is as it is !!!

64

Vowel recognition

Explain to the child that five of the letters he has already learned are special letters called vowels. Introduce them now:

a   e   i   o   u

Help him learn that "Vowels are pals." Tell him that vowels are very hard-workers. It is impossible to have a word without using at least one of these five vowel letters.

Read the funny vowel sentences on the next two pages to the child, pointing to each vowel as you go.

Short Vowels (1)

Short vowels say, "Elephants itch octopuses under apple tree.s"

e **e**lephants

i **i**tch

o **o**ctopuses

u **u**nder

a **a**pple trees

Short Vowels (2)

Short vowels also say, "Ants exist on undercooked inchworms."

a **a**nts

e **e**xist

o **o**n

u **u**ndercooked

i **i**nchworms

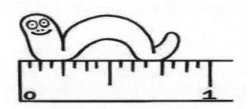

"Slide-a-vowel" word maker stick

Preparation of the stick:

Photocopy this page. Cut out the two vowel rectangles and tape them, back to back, onto a 3x5 card. Cut the 3x5 card down to the same size as the vowel rectangles. Affix this stiff slice of card onto a popsicle stick, a plastic knife or an emery fingernail file.

Using the stick:

Slide the vowel stick into the middle of each three-letter word (on the following pages) to make more words to decode. Have the child read and say aloud the words this creates.

By the way: you will now encounter a different font of "a"—used in all printed matter (rather than the "ɑ"). Likewise, the "ɡ" has changed to a "g."

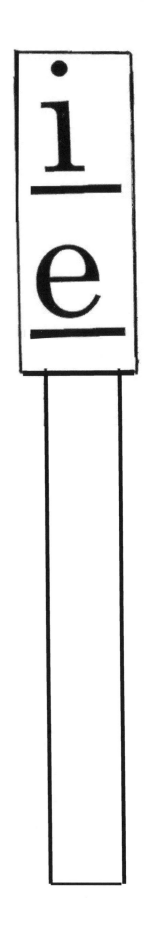

b a g

h a t

t a n

g t

ban

bad

pat

only uses a, o and u

cab

only uses a, o, and u

cap

only uses a, i, and o

had

only uses a, e, i, and o

sat

mad

m a t

only uses i, o and u

r   b

p a n

only uses a, o, and u

c a t

only uses a and o

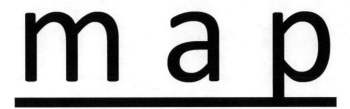

m a p

doesn't use o

p   g

only uses a, e, i, and u

f a n

only uses i, o, and u

d   g

only uses a, i, and o

f a x

only uses a, e, and i

l a d

b a t

only uses a, i, o, and u

t a p

b a ll

doesn't use i

b a ss

n t

d ll

only uses a, i, and u

d a d

only uses a and i

z a p

h a m

r a c k

<u>pap</u>

<u>lag</u>

doesn't use e

<u>sack</u>

<u>dan</u>

doesn't use e

lack

only uses a and i

lap

only uses a, i and o

wag

only uses e and o

n   d

3-letter word test

Photocopy the following three-letter word test—or just have the child point to the correct answer with the eraser end of a pencil or smooth end of a pen.

Call out any one of the three words in each three-word group to see if the child circles the correct one. When the child has finished the test, go back and re-teach each word missed and then administer the test again until the majority of his answers are correct.

The pictures have nothing to do with the words. They merely identify which row the child is to be on.

Student Phonics Sounds Test #2   (for each three-word set, circle the word you heard the teacher say)

(knife)	(clock)	(truck)	(fish)	(horn)	(button)	(cup)	(dress)	(boot)	(glass)	(sun)
dig	ned	pup	sat	cat	ban	bag	pen	bell	pot	nat
dog	nod	ned	set	cut	bed	beg	pin	bill	put	net
dug	hut	nod	sit	cot	bin	big	pon	boll	get	not
had	dad	tug	cap	map	bun	bog	pun	bull	git	nit
hid	did	ted	cop	mop	wag	bug	bad	dell	got	nut
hed	dud	tog	cup	met	wig	bat	bed	dill	gut	mat
don	tap	lap	peg	dan	cab	bet	bid	doll	mad	mit
din	tip	lip	pig	den	cob	bit	bod	dull	mud	mot
dun	top	lag	pug	din	cub	tun	bud	pan	met	mut
zap	fan	leg	pep	rib	lad	ham	tan	fax	hat	pat
zip	fin	log	pip	rob	led	hem	ten	fix	hit	pet
zup	fun	lug	pop	rub	lid	him	tin	fox	hot	pit

Capital letter charts

Teach these exactly as you did the lowercase letters. Teaching six letters at a time, tap on the starting dot or number, trace and then test on the plain letters chart, immediately following, to see what the child retains.

You'll notice that the letters c, o, s, v, w, x, and z have been eliminated—because their capital shapes are the same as their lowercase shapes.

Be sure to say the phonetic sound and trigger word as you go, just like you did when teaching the tracing of the lowercase letters.

apple

baby

dog

elephant

fix

give

82

A a apple

B b baby

D d dog

E e elephant

F f fix

G g give

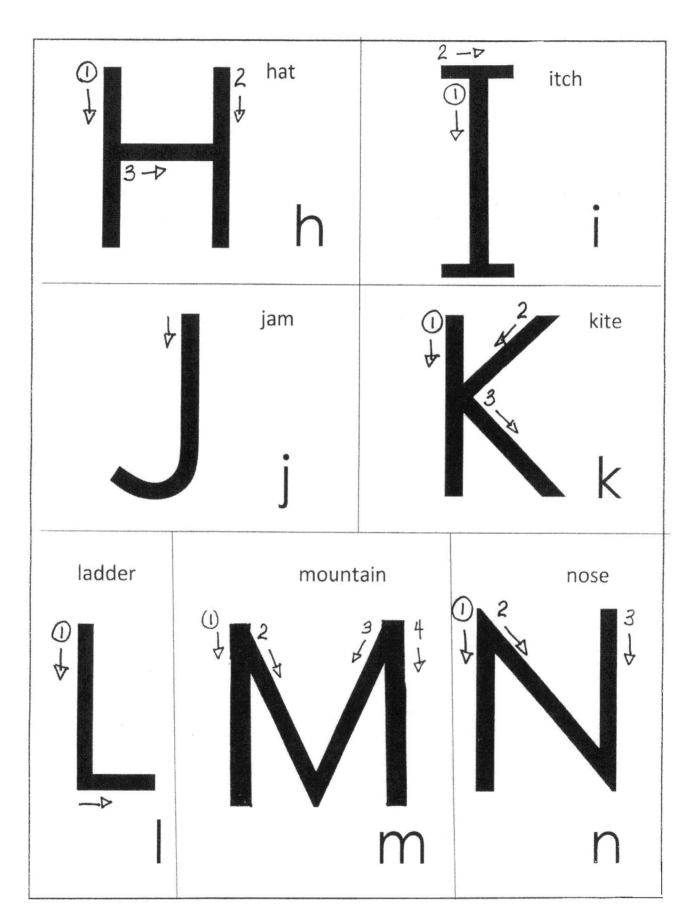

hat

h

itch

i

jam

j

kite

k

ladder

l

mountain

m

nose

n

84

H h hat

I i itch

J j jam

K k kite

L l ladder

M m mountain

N n nose

85

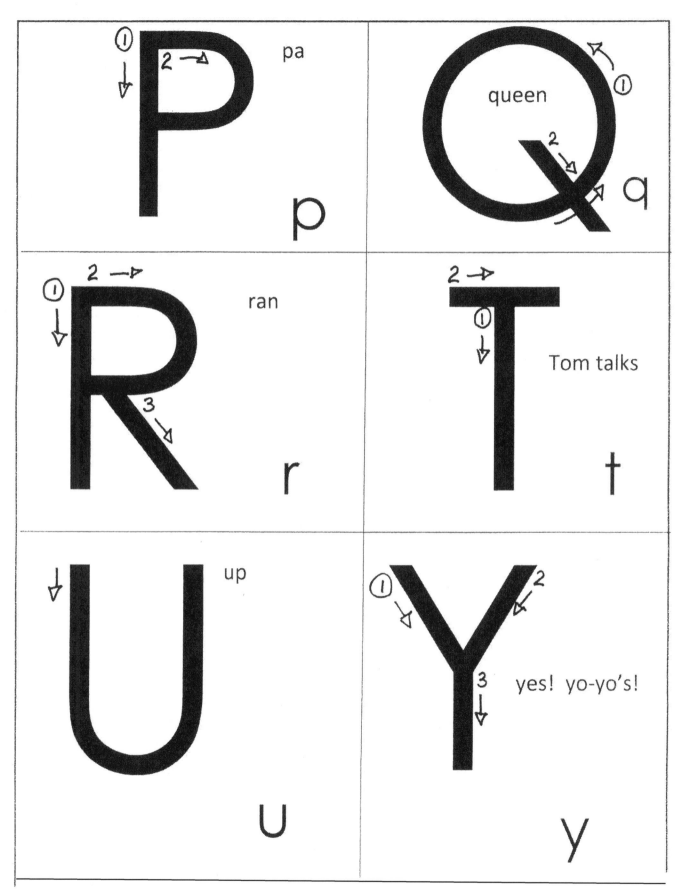

P pa p

Q queen q

R ran r

T Tom talks t

U up u

Y yes! yo-yo's! y

P ^{pa} p

Q queen q

R ^{ran} r

T Tom talks t

U ^{up} u

Y yes! yo-yo's! y

Finger tracking—to avoid getting lost

Teach the student to finger track all of his beginning reading. In early reading, a child will often get ahead of himself and lose the vital one-to-one correspondence of letter/sound alliance. This causes him to totally lose his place. Often when this happens a child will continue to read a few words more by "context" alone—i.e. by guesswork, not de-coding. To avoid this, in the beginning have the child always proceed to read by placing his pointer finger under each letter of the word as he says each of the sounds.

Teach your student to hold onto one sound verbally until he meets the next sound. As he completes the letters found in a word, have him immediately go back to the beginning of that word to slide his finger quickly under the whole word, while saying it again, blending the sounds more smoothly the second time. Maintain this practice until he develops some fluency and can read without this letter-by-letter guidance.

In the beginning, if the child is very young or does not have much dexterity of his own, YOU track for him using the eraser end of a pencil, the smooth end of a pen, or a chopstick. Eventually you can use a 3x5 card (with its lower long edge flipped up ½ inch as a handle), setting it under a whole row of words and dragging it down the page from row to row.

Silly sentences

Each of these sentences uses controlled, short-vowel, three-letter words.

First use:
Help your child read a page of silly sentences a day—either all in one sitting or spaced over several sessions, if your child tires.

Whenever you encounter the word "the," treat it as a sight word and say it aloud for the child.

Second use:
Return to these sentences AFTER the child has read through all of the silly **stories**, too, AND has completed all of the handwriting exercises. Now you will use these sentences again to DICTATE them, as the child writes them. Complete one sentence a day while continuing on with the further phonics exercises contained in the remainder of this book, at the same time.

Dictation is a marvelous tool for reinforcing your teaching. It reveals what is making its way into the student's actual usage. Can he spell what he hears, and can he do the punctuation correctly?

During dictation, change your voice quality when you need to indicate punctuation. Also, spell out the word "the" for the child, each time it is encountered.

To add more fun, children can illustrate some of these with stick figures sketches, if they are so inclined.

Rub wet rags on bad rugs.

The dull lad led cats up hills.

The pug bit the cat in the gut.

Did the sun nod and set?

Rob not the man!

Rags in bags will sag.

The dog has not fins and bills.

Sit and sip and sup.

Dan can run zig zag.

Sal did sob.

Sid put lids on the pans.

Hem his hat!

Zap the ham 2 Pam.

 Ten bugs lit up.

Hug Jan.

Tom got tan.

Fax the tax!

he fox did fix him.

Jim is hot and mad!

A wet pet sits in the pig pen.

The cup tips.

Cal hit his hip, and bit his lip.

Men lug logs and tin.

Sin not, Tom!

 Zap wet on the mud hen.

Fan the hot man.

Pigs put cobs in mud.

Pip, the dog, had pep.

Pop the can.

Put the bill on the sill.

Bad men did not win.

Hun, put the bun in the pan.

1 hip has 1 leg.

The bell did tell "all is well."

The cats and dogs bit the ribs.

Pat the pet in the pit.

Don is at the top.

Tap the hot pot, not!

Win the lap dog.

In the din did sit Jim.

A doll is fun, Jill!

Did cubs sit in the tub?

A bad leg is not fun.

"Bag it" and beg!

Cops nab bad cabs.

The mob sins and sobs.

The tub had suds and suds.

Dull Jill sat on the hill.

Did top Jan win?

Pens and pins sit in bins.

Ban the bad man!

Zip his lip!

Bud and Sal met.

Get the pot and the pan
  2 the man.

Net the pet, not!

Hug the pet, yes!

Put the nut in the cup.

Nab the mat and sit.

The fun dog did dig and jig.

Fit Jim ran and won

Ned sat in bed and did nod.

Jeb ran laps in the tub.

The cat did sit on the cot.

In the bin sat sad Kim.

Get the jet 2 run.

The wet rag sat on the red ball.

The fat fox got the sad cat.

Kit bit the tip of the mitt.

The hot pan did tip!

The gob of cubs met.

The dog got mad at the pig.

 Dad hid.

Get Jim peg legs.

Al did fib.

Sal had ten ribs!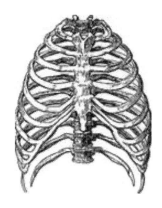

The sad dog did dig sod.

The mud hit the fan.

Did he get his "hip hat" off
the top of the hot hill?

The mad cop set the
big dog in the red car.

Ned and Ben set 4
hens on 8 hot eggs.

Ten men set the tan ox on
the red box.

Funny stories

The only **sight word** needed to read these stories is again the word "the". Teach the child the SHAPE of this word (a triangle △); draw as little attention to the actual letters of "the" as possible.

In addition, we have temporarily added several phonetically consistent **substitutions** to give early reading more variety. They are:

... **"uv"**, which substitutes for the word "of". This innocent departure will be corrected later; it includes the correct spelling subliminally even now, in these examples.

...the **number 2** is used in place of the short word "to" because "to" doesn't use the octopus sound for "o" and hasn't been introduced as another sight word, yet, either.

...**b-4** is used to replace "before". Be sure, though, to only pronounce it "buh-4" (with a southern accent!) as we have not yet introduced the letter NAME of "bee" for "b" (buh) yet.

..."**um**" has been substituted for "them" in just one or two cases.

Sentences used in these stories:
...**represent very CONTROLLED VOCABULARY**, which promotes increased confidence in acquiring early reading skill.

...**avoid the use of the isolated "a"** as in "a" cat, "a" dog, etc. because its isolated sound (neither its short vowel sound nor its long vowel sound) has not been introduced yet. In its isolated usage THIS "a" sounds like "uh" as in "a-lone" or "a-part".

..**also avoid the use of the capital "I"** as in "I sit", because that, too represents the long "I" sound ("i" as in ice), which we have not yet introduced.

Bud and His Tub

Bud got in the big jet tub and had suds. But tons uv [of] bad bugs in the tub ran up the wall and got on Bud. Bud sat on the bugs and put his red rag on the suds. And in the end, wet Bud set the hot fan on him. Bud did win and top the bugs and suds!

The Pet Dog

The lad led his mad pet to bed. But it ran zip and zag. His pet pug had a fit and bit the leg uv [of] the bed. The lad had it. Rob NOT the bed! It will sag. And the bed bag will sag, 2. The bill and tax will set in. Pip, the pet, will not wag but will sit in its bin and sob.

Put a lid on it, pug!

Not, Not

Dull men sip tin cups of hot gin. Ban it. Sit on hips. Zip up lips. Zap the will. Tip not the cup. And "All is well!"   All is tops!

Jeb Runs and Runs

Jeb ran laps. Did not sit in laps and did not nap.
On the cot, Jeb is not. Jeb is tip-top. Jeb wins and tells laps did it, not nods and naps.

The Rag-Tag-Man and Hogs

Hug the man and hem his hat and hem his bag. Hem his ten tan tops. 2 not fix the "rag-tag-man" will put him in the pen and will run the hens and pigs of [off]. Set gobs of cobs and ribs b-4 him, 2, 2 fill him up. Fix him!

2 Kids

2 kids sat up on the hill. Did the ball fall in the lap "uv" [of] Jen? Ken had a hat, but Ken did set it on the hill. Jen hit the ball at the hat. Yes, it hit! Ken put gum on the hat and on the ball 2. The kids had fun!

 # 2 Gals

Lil and Jill, as gals and pals, did not ham it up. Sam, the pet, did ham it up. Sam had pep. Sam sat sod in the lap uv [of] Lil and put cans of pop on the top uv Jill. Lil got mad. Jill got ill. Bad Sam.

2 Men

Tom and Ben had tons uv [of] jobs. Pull and lug logs. Lug and pull.

Set buns in pans and get em [them] hot. Put the buns in the tum-tums. Yum! Yum!

The Sun Is Hot

The sun is hot, hot, hot.

The hen sits in the hut.

The mutt beds on top of the hut.

The cat did nap and sag on the hut. The 3 did not run!

The Pup

The pup did tap on the hat.

The pup sat in the hat.

The pup bit and did rip the hat.

The hat had "had it!"

The pup got put in the pen.

Bad pup.

An Act Not 2 Do!

If an eg [egg] is up in a box on an ox, it will sit in the sun and get hot. But the fox will run and beg 2 sup on the eg, and get up on the ox. The bull will run and beg, 2. And the dog and cat and bat will run up on the ox 2 sup. But if the fox and bull and dog and cat and bat tip and fall of [off] the ox, it is not fun to sup on an ox!

The pals did get of [off] the ox b-4 the ox got up. The eg did not get up and fell of [off] in the box. Yes, the sun and ox did up, up, up! Sad eg.

Introducing long vowels

Keep in mind, when beginning this step, that we've already taught the short vowel sounds by assigning that first sound to them in the letter cartoons (as if it were the vowel's ONLY sound) right along with each consonant's only sound. The child saw no difference between the vowels and the consonants. They were learned together, and they each had only one sound.

In this next step we finally make the student aware that five of the letters are special letters called vowels. Explain that vowel letters are special because they are HARD WORKERS. A person cannot make (and/or read) a word without at least one vowel in it.

Explain that vowels have TWO sounds for the same letter. One sound is called the short vowel sound, and is marked above the letter with a smile. The other long vowel sound is marked with a dash above the letter, and is called the long vowel sound.

We use smiles above the short vowel sounds, because the student already knows those sounds. The long sideways dash over a long vowel not only alerts him to its new alphabet name but also helps him remember that he says and holds that new, different sound for a longer duration than he held the short vowel sound for that same letter.

On the following page is an example of how one letter can make two different sounds.

Same mother—
2 different names:

Mŏm   Jōan

Same letter—
2 different sounds:

Ŏ   Ō

Hearing long vowel words

Have your student repeat (echo) the words on these long vowel lists after you. Point to the vowel with the eraser end of a pencil as you say all the words in that list. Exaggerate and hold the vowel sound for a longer duration than the rest of the word. Have the child echo you, saying each word exactly the way you said it—right after you.

ā	ē
āngel	ēēls
āpron	ēagle
ācorn	ēleven
āpricot	ēvening
ā	ēasel
āge	ēat

ī	ō	ū
īvy	ōatmeal	ūnicorn
īsland	ōveralls	Ūnited States
īcicles	ōnly	ūnicycle
ī	ōvercōat	ūnit
īdea	ōpen	ūse
īce crēam	ōld	ūniform

Long Vowels (1)
Long vowels say, "Apes eat only useless ice!!"

ā **a**pes

ē **e**at

ō **o**nly

ū **u**seless

ī **i**ce

Long Vowels (2)
Long vowels also say, "Usually I only eat cake."

Ū **us**ually

Ī **i**

Ō **o**nly

Ē **e**at

Ā **ca**ke

Learning vowel markings

On the following page, note the difference in the short and long vowel sounds and markings. You as the parent/teacher say the words in the two columns, reading horizontally, across the page, as you point to each. First read the short vowel word and its isolated sound, and then the long vowel word with its isolated sound.

Vowel markings

short vowels	long vowels
ă	ā
apples	ape
ĕ	ē
elephant	eat
ĭ	ī
itch	ice
ŏ	ō
odd	only
ŭ	ū
up	useless

How to read long vowels

**If a vowel has a dash,
change its sound fast.
Read long vowels true,
by thinking "dessert menu"**

long ā   a plate of 8
         is what I ate!

long ē   EZ treats
         is what I eats!

long ī   ice cream I'm eyein'
         while rice I am fryin'

long ō   to open the oats
         is what I hopes!
         (think oatmeal cookies)

long ū   you use a tube
         to unify food
         (think blender)

Transitioning to reading long vowels

Fortunately, there is a CLUE built right into a word, as to when to read that vowel as a long vowel sound, instead of a short vowel sound. The clue is found in this simple rhyme:

**"When two vowels go walking
the first one does the talking!"**

Have the student memorize this ditty.

Explain that in any word with two vowels, the first vowel will say its long vowel sound—its actual alphabet name— and the second vowel will be silent.

This is true whether the second vowel sits right next to the first vowel or is separated by a consonant letter in between.

To actually learn to apply this two-vowel concept, initially we must work the student through many examples of it so that he will become competent with reading it fluently.

Instead of slowly wading through complete sentences to note such examples, we toss the student into a veritable sea of examples right away: 160 of them! We work through hem in groups of five—only one group of five words per session, over several sessions per day.

Photocopy the eight pages of vowel sound recognition exercises that follow the vowel train explanation page. Then, guide the student to use his pencil to cross out the silent vowel, in every case, and put a long vowel dash over the vowel that IS pronounced. Next, have him contrast his long vowel word with the short vowel version of the "same" word, immediately to his left in the list, and put a smile on top of the vowel (a short vowel symbol) on that already known vowel. Finally, have the student read both words aloud.

By seeing so many examples of both the short vowel word and its long vowel version side by side, the student masters this further decoding strategy, rapidly.

First, let's show you how to build a vowel train...

Make yourself a vowel train

As an added incentive to your student, you may want to turn the "long vowel marking exercise" on the following pages into a vowel train! Have your student only work through one set of five word combinations at a time. You can do several boxes of these sets a day if you space them out—one in the morning, one in the afternoon and one in the evening, for example.

You'll make the train out of 33 (3x5) index cards. Draw a boxcar and two wheels on each card with a black marker, as you go. If you want the card train to be heavier, attach ¾ inch washers (purchased from a hardware store) to each boxcar—over its drawn wheels.

Tape the cards together on the short three-inch ends, as you add to them each day. In other words, don't make the train all at once in the beginning; build it as you go. Then, each day, tape the day's finished group of five words into each boxcar. (Fold it in half first, with the words facing out. The top will stick out over the top edge of the 3x5 cards—as if the words are coal cargo or overflowing lumber.)

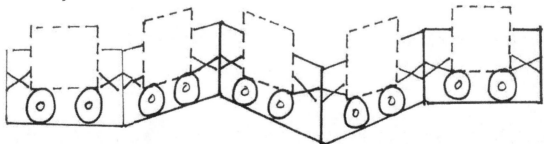

Add several boxcars (with the day's finished exercises) each day until you've finished with all 33 sets. Fold up the train to store it when you're done each day—or stretch it down the length of a hallway wall, so the child can watch it "grow!".

răn – rāin

bed – bead

got – goat

cot – coat

fet – feet

răk – rāke

lef – leaf

rack – rake

kit – kite

mad–made

bon – bone

bik – bike

fir – fire

nos – nose

pi – pie

can – cane

Jan – Jane

pal – pail

man–mane

at – ate

wep – weep	cub – cube
net – neat	not – note
pat – pate	bit – bite
bot – boat	cak – cake
rop – rope	ross – rose
Sam – same	bak – bake
gat – gate	nam – name
mat – mate	rag – rage
lat – late	fed – feed
mal – mail	set – seat

bep – beep	Ted – tea
bet – beet	bat – bait
rud – rude	tack – take
ten – teen	sek – seek
sack – sake	hid – hide
pock – poke	den – Dean
gal – gale	red – read
lad – laid	pet – Pete
pad – paid	fit – fite
wad – wade	het – heat

duck – duke	Ned–need
pan – pain	wed–weed
tam – tame	kep – keep
cav – cave	kin – kine
dav – Dave	lep – leap
dim – dime	lik – like
rip – ripe	mil – mile
fin – fine	nin – nine
fill – file	bib – bibe
hiv – hive	div – dive

hop – hope	luck – Luke
bat – bate	dun – dune
Jon – Joan	mutt–mute
rod – road	sut – Sue
Todd – toad	lit – lite
did – died	grap–grape
lin – line	sop – soap
zip – zipe	cod – code
tin – tine	doll – dole
fiv – five	Sid – side

pin – pine	bad–bade
Sal – sail	bin – bine
tal – tale	us – use
wip – wipe	tub – tube
pill – pile	cut – cute
hat – hate	van – vane
fat – fate	con – cone
rat – rate	gap – gape
Al – ale	tap – tape
fad – fade	bass–base

ban – bane	lop – lope
god – goad	cop – cope
mack–make	mop–mope
back – bake	Rob – robe
lack – lake	tot – tote
cap – cape	dick – dike
Jack – Jake	win – wine
ap – ape	bid – bide
dat – date	din – dine
dud – dude	met –meet

et – eat	rub – rube
led – lead	cob – cobe
Tim – time	lam – lame
met – meat	wok–wake
mill – mile	bef – beef
peck – peek	sen – seen
ab – abe	bod –bode
bill – bile	ad – ade
cat – Kate	dad– Dade
dop – dope	dot – dote

Why include printing HERE, in the midst of READING?

We incorporate printing/beginning penmanship in this phonics program in the midst of teaching a child how to read because it additionally embeds recognition of the shape of the letter/symbol through touch/feel. It takes the tracing step one step further. If the child can print the letter perfectly (i.e., he knows both the starting point and the directions of each stroke), it stands to reason that he has visually internalized every detail about that letter.

When you've finished with these printing exercises you can then go back and begin dictating the three-letter silly sentences, for further practice.

Printing keeps the letter (and/or whole words) from remaining a vague impression or a foggy approximation. This dual-cognitive imprinting of both sight and touch allows the student to lodge the symbol (or full word) in both hemispheres of the brain, thus strengthening reading mastery and fluency.

Important:

From this stage forward you'll be doing two things per session:

- a printing page and
- continuing the reading exercises from page 147 onward.

Directions for learning to print

Until now, your student has only traced letters with the smooth clicker end of a pen. In this next section he now begins to actually print with a pencil.

We start learning to print using one-inch graph paper because it accurately teaches the total geography (North, South, East and West) of each letter. This trains the child in how much space each letter takes up in proportion to itself, helping him to eventually form the numbers and letters correctly in any new setting, later.

To begin with, make photocopies of each of the following practice pages. Have the child trace over a graph-paper number/letter with his pencil, and then actually print that letter/number again in the blank space(s) next to and/or below each one.

You will note that in this practice section we move from large spaces to smaller spaces. If the child is very young or has poor dexterity, avoid the smaller space exercises for now. Pick them up again later.

Make sure the student forms the letters and numbers accurately, by carefully hovering over this beginning stage. Stay right with him for the formation of each and every symbol, because you are training lifetime habits here. If you don't carefully coach now, at this stage, it will be much more difficult later to undo any bad habits that developed outside of your watchful eye. Give it all the coaching NOW that it needs.

Learn to print numbers

Make several photocopies of this page and have your student learn to trace these numbers now using a pencil.

To teach the concept of how MANY objects/dots the numbers 2, 3, 4 and 5 represent in the concrete world, you can show him that you simply count the number of end points of the printed number— they turn into counting dots!

Count the dots:

2. 3. 4. 5.

1	2	3	4	5
6	7	8	9	☺

Tips for teaching the printing of numbers

(photocopy the following page first)

- The top halves of the numbers 3, 4, 5 and 8 must sit on the center line of the square. We have included dashes in the empty squares to ensure that this happens.

- The traditional method for teaching how to print a 5 is to begin with making a little capital letter L. That L must sit on the center line of the square.

- An 8 is made with an S and then a straight stick drawn from the bottom of the end of the S to the starting point of the S at the top. Both the S and the stick returning home must pass through the same center dot.

Trace, then print below the number.

1 2 3 4 5 6 7 8

---- ---- ----   ----

9 0 1 2 3 4 5 6

---- ---- ----

7 8 9 0 1 2 3 4

---- ---- ----

5 6 7 8 9 0 8 9

---- ---- ----

Printing numbers in half-inch squares
(photocopy the following page first)

In addition to learning to write numbers well here, try providing this ½ inch sized graph paper for all future math work (this can be ordered from Miller Pads and Paper or on Amazon). If you do, it will result in clearer, more accurate thinking and far fewer mistakes for your student, well into the future. Remember to photocopy this master sheet before having the student begin this printing exercise.

1	2	3	4	5	6	7
8	9	0	1	2	3	4
5	6	7	8	9	0	1
2	3	4	5	6	7	8
9	0	1	2	3	4	5
6	7	8	9	0	1	2

Straight stick letters

Before making the "w" each time, make 3 dots on the top of the square and 2 dots on the
bottom of the square. Then, photocopy this sheet. Have the student trace each letter on
his photocopy and print it in *all* of the available squares surrounding it.

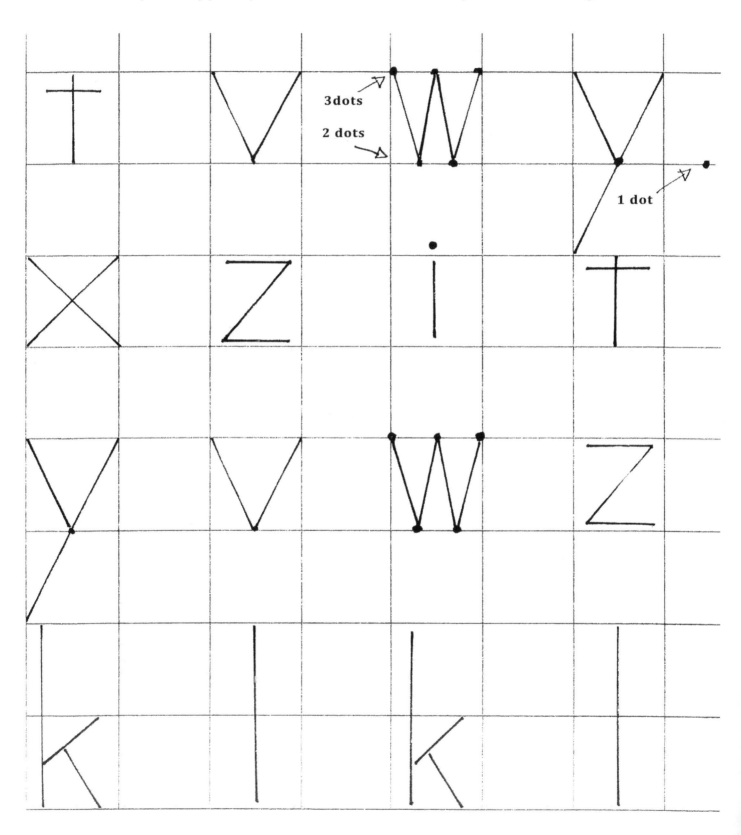

Trace and print in all available spaces.

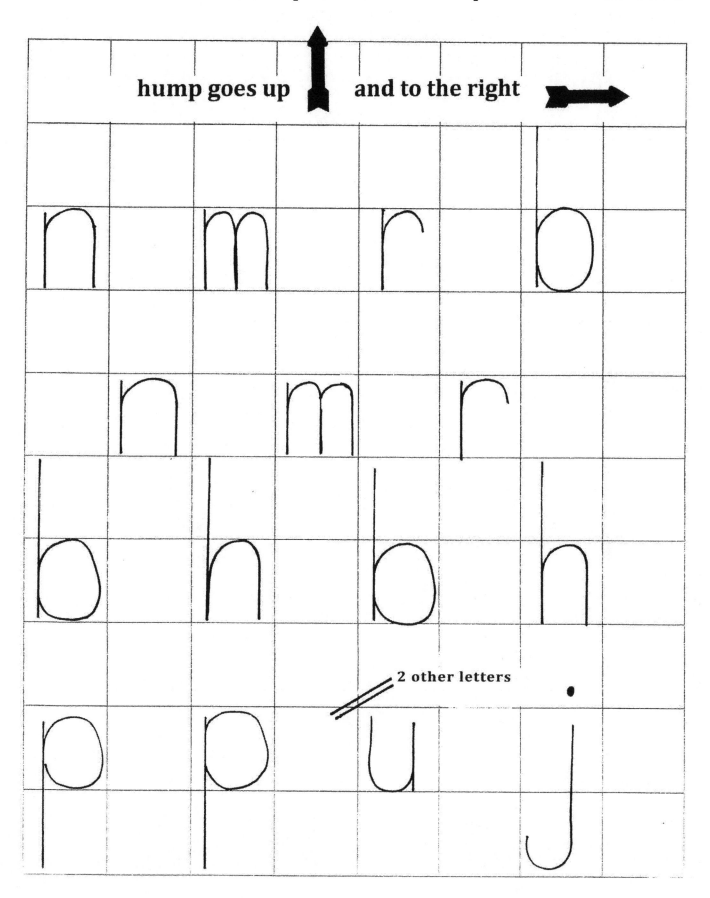

hump goes up and to the right

2 other letters

All left hump letters on the following pages begin at 2 o'clock and are printed counterclockwise.

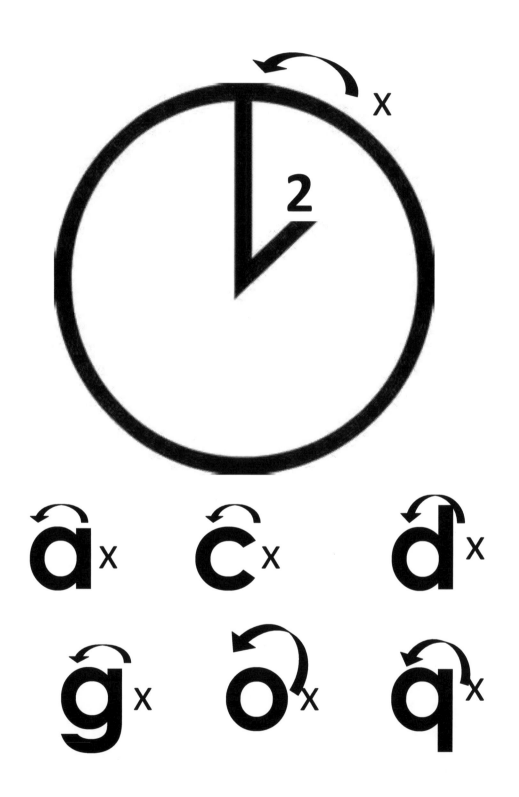

hump goes up ↑ and to the left ←

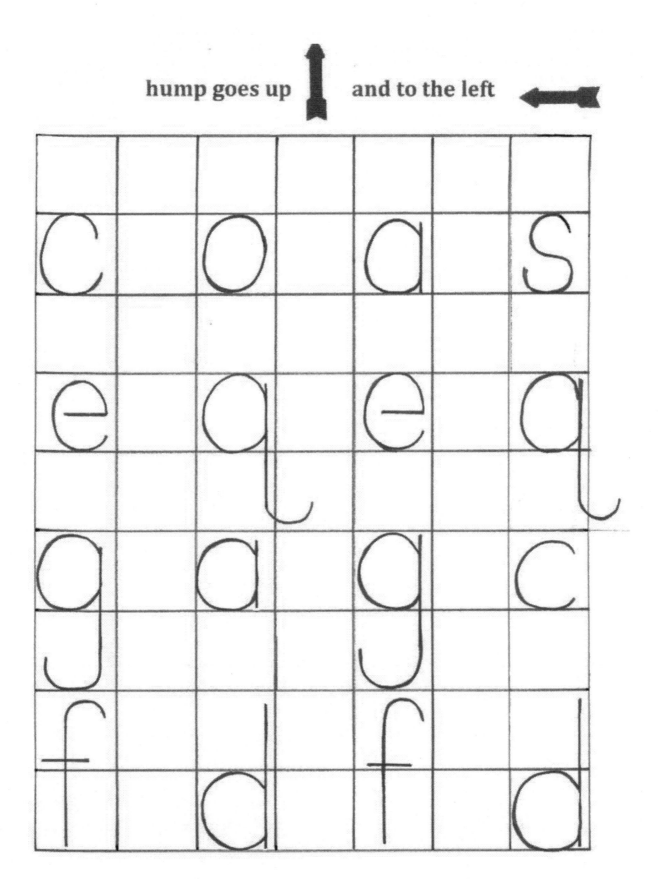

c		o		a		s
e		q		e		a
g		a		g		c
f		d		f		d

Trace these letters

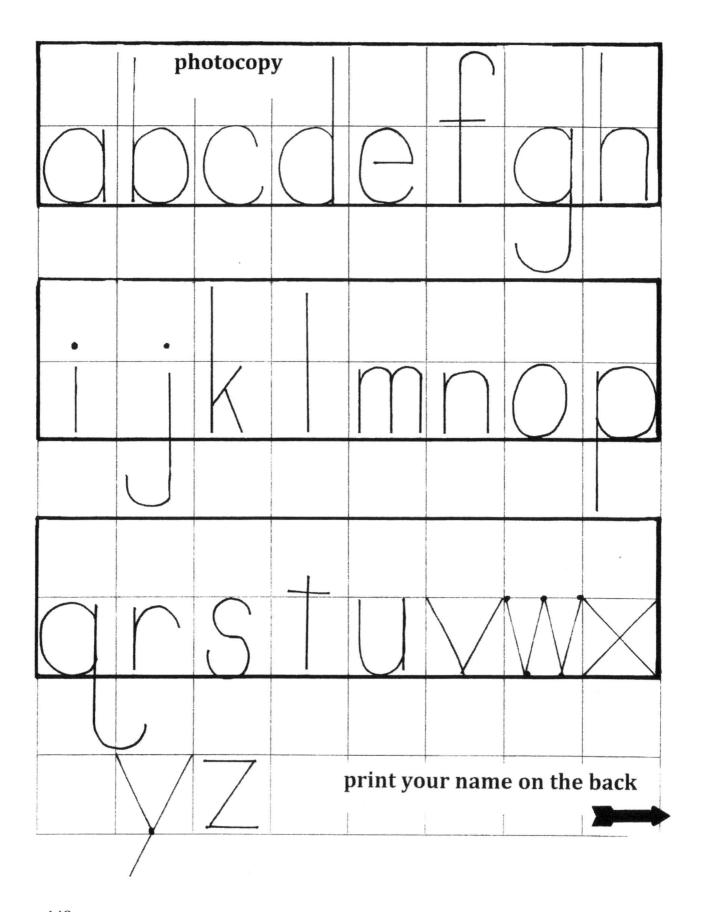

photocopy

a b c d e f g h

i j k l m n o p

q r s t u v w x

y z

print your name on the back

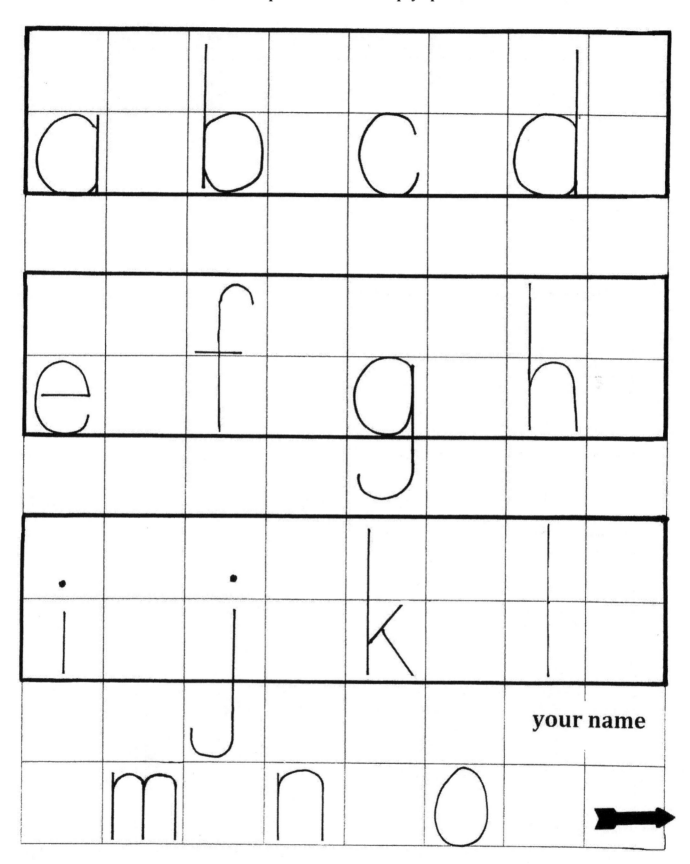

your name

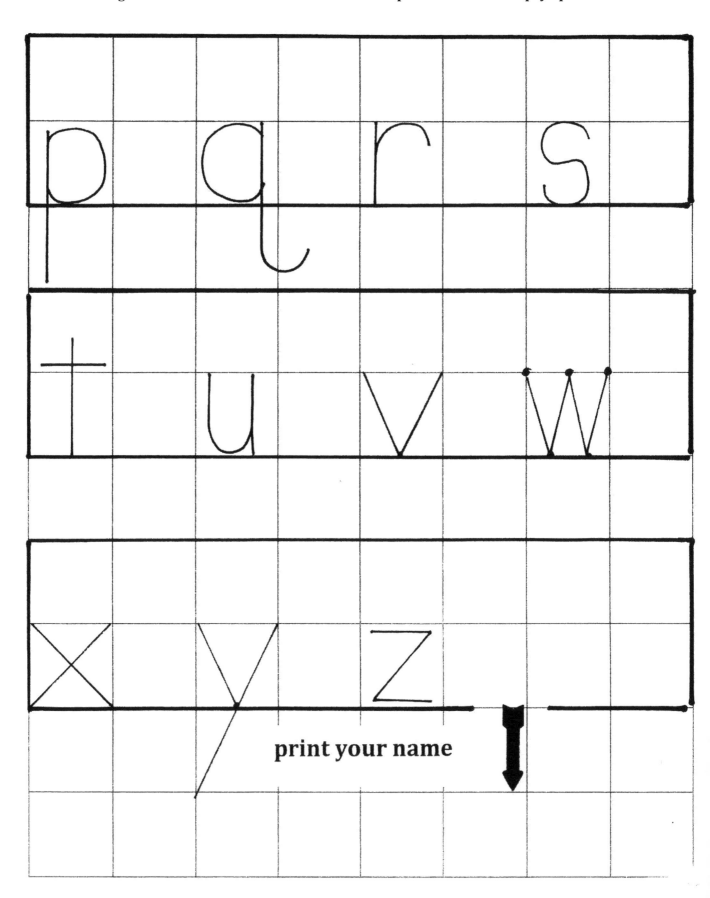

p q r s

t u v w

x y z

print your name

A	B	D	E
F	G	H	I
J	K	L	M
N	P	Q	R
T	U	Y	

Trace and print in all the empty spaces

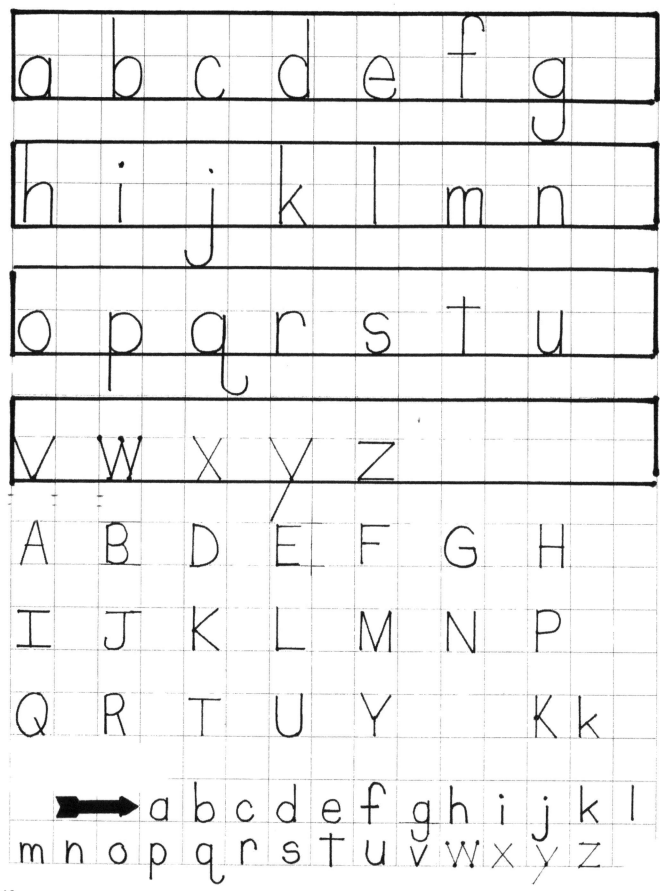

More phonics

This last section of phonics is taught alongside the preceding pages of printing exercises. Each reading session with the child from here on out will have two parts: the printing drill and these further phonics drills. The phonics now cover sight words, blends, and irregular words of several sorts.

Building from regular to irregular words, as you have done in this course, builds decoding confidence.

The fact that you are now at this part of the book shows that you have diligently worked through all of the beginning parts and that your child IS now reading well on some level. Congratulations!

The following two pages deal with the **four most common sight words**. These words can't be decoded; they must be memorized. Therefore, drill them well.

of

says "uv"

(on top "of" each step)

to

very short
and says "tu"

a

the

the book
the bag
the boy

"a" stands "a-lone,"
"a-part" from others

Sight Word Drill
(the 4 most frequently used sight words)

the	of	a	to
to	a	the	of
the	to	of	a
of	a	to	the
a	to	the	of
to	the	of	a

Blends

Exposure (first 2 pages)

Say each blend (and its sample word after it) on the next two pages, as you point to the blend only. Have the child echo you (i.e., say) each blend after you, as you go. Point to each one (using the eraser end of a pencil) as you move along.

Practice, with pictures (8 pages)

On pages 153-160 look at just one group of four pictures at a time. Tell the child the name of each picture, before doing the matching drill. To begin the first drill, cover up the bottom half of the page with blank paper. Working just the top half, using eight U.S. quarters, or eight buttons, have the child cover up each blend and each picture as he matches them up by pointing to them both. Repeatedly ask the question "Which picture starts with.... ____"? (and then you name a blend). The word below the blend is for the parent to KNOW, not to say. The parent only says the blend. Continue until all four written blends and all four pictures are covered with coins. Next, cover up the top half of the page with blank paper and repeat the exercise with the lower four pictures and blends.

Mastery (return to the first 2 pages)

Cover up the bottom two-thirds of the first pages of lists with blank paper, so that only the top third of the page with four blends shows. Test by asking "Which one says?" randomly, and again cover the done blends (the letters only, not the words) with the coins, until all four are covered. Then continue with the next four, and finally the bottom four, this time covering the top of the page with blank paper.

Finally, test the whole page randomly, again using the coins. First, you say the blend and the child points. Then do the opposite. This time YOU point and the child says the blend sound, himself. If he does not pass this test, then go back and re-do the picture practice pages.

Blends
(2 consonants together that make one sound)

bl	black	**dr**	drag
br	brick	**fl**	fly
ch	chair	**fr**	frog
ck	duck	**gl**	glue
cl	clock	**gr**	green
cr	crib	**ph**	"f" phone

pl	plant	**sn**	snow
pr	prince	**sp**	spill
sc	scarf	**st**	star
sch	school	**sw**	swing
sh	sheep	**th**	thumb
sk	skirt	**tr**	truck
sl	sled	**tw**	twin
sm	smile	**wh**	whale

cr	**sn**	**sl**	**gl**
crab	snail	sled	glue
ph	**sh**	**fl**	**br**
phone	sheep	flag	brick

cl	gr	sl	gl
clock	green tree	slug	glove

pl	bl	cl	sh
plug	bloom	clam	ship

154

dr	**sk**	**sp**	**pr**
drop	skirt	spider	present
st	**gl**	**tw**	**sm**
steps	glass	twins	smile

gr grill

sl slippers

fr fruit

cl cloud

mop

pl plate

fl floor

br bridge

br brush

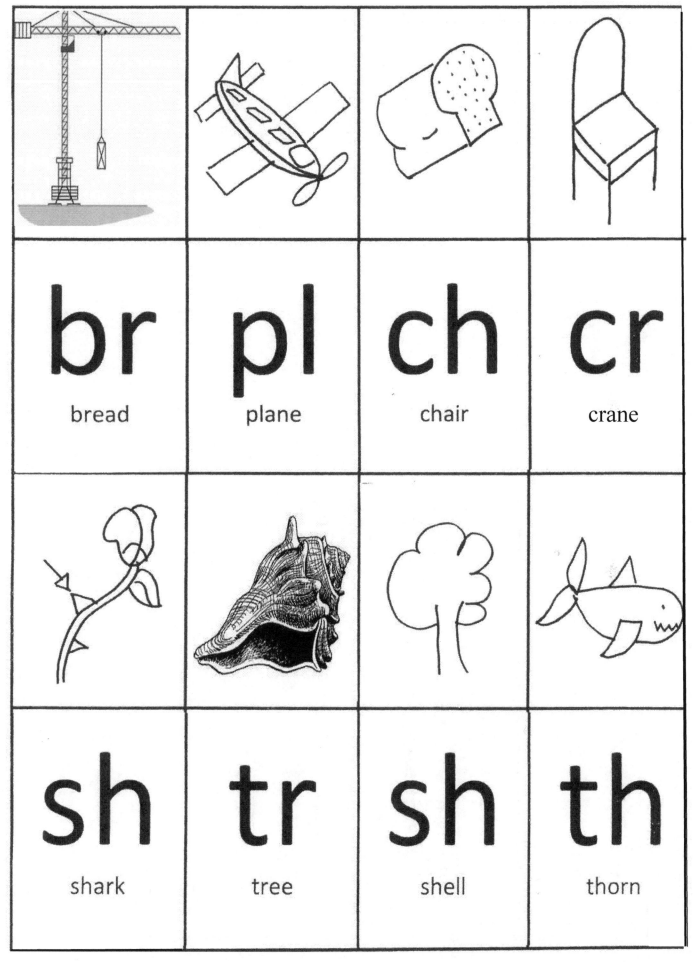

| br | pl | ch | cr |
| bread | plane | chair | crane |

| sh | tr | sh | th |
| shark | tree | shell | thorn |

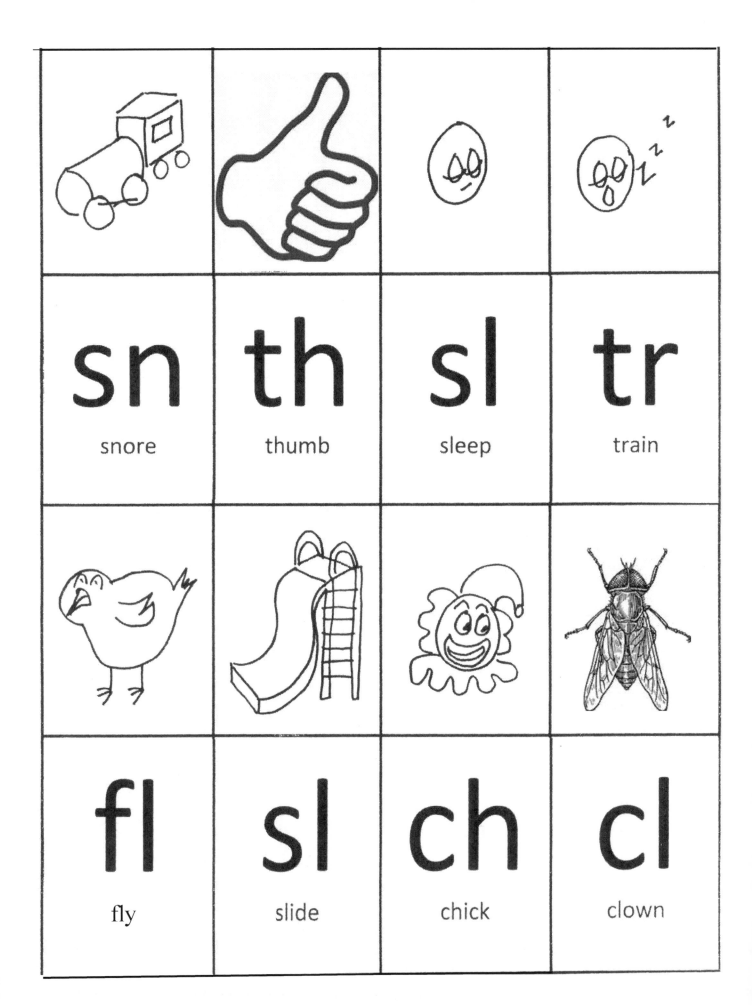

sn	**th**	**sl**	**tr**
snore	thumb	sleep	train
fl	**sl**	**ch**	**cl**
fly	slide	chick	clown

wh	**cr**	**pl**	**sn**
whale	crust	plant	snowflake
gl	**cr**	**wh**	**fr**
globe	crib	wheel	frog

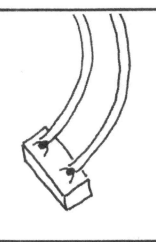

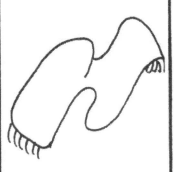

st

stove

sc

scarf

sk

skunk

sw

swing

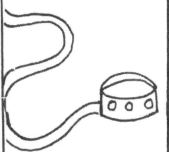

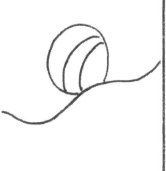

Ending Blends

ck

duck

ch

beach

sh

leash

sh

fish

More sight words

What is a sight word?

A sight word is a word that cannot be decoded using standard phonetic rules. It must be learned by visual memory frequency, instead (i.e., drilled as a sight word).

For example:
The word "we" defies phonetic decoding attack of any sort. If one were to use the short "e" sound, which we usually do with such a word, we would produce a clipped "whiff" of a sound—which doesn't say "we" at all. On the other hand, if we were to use the long "e" vowel sound rule, the word would need to be spelled "wee"... hmmm, that still doesn't help us.

The total number of actual sight words is fewer than most publishers indicate. Many words that are listed as sight words—even in sight word flashcard packets—*can* be sounded out using phonetic rules. A real sight word cannot.

How to teach for mastery:

What follows is a list of the most common basic sight words. Photocopy the lists and cut out each word. Tape each individual word onto a 3x5 card. After attaching the words onto cards, you can then cover the face of each card with contact paper or clear packing tape to give each card a glossy feel and to protect the cards from damage through multiple uses.

Proceed to drill a few words at a time, three times a day. To double-benefit your time doing this drill you can use meal times to provide quick multiple reviews. After introducing each little batch of words, you may find that you have good success learning the words if you set the individual cards around the house in unexpected places. The child "finds" the word, runs to you with the card, and SAYS with you the word that's on the card. Another game you can play, after introducing them, is to set out three sight word cards at a time and ask, "Which one says _____?"

to

too

two

of

off

it's

its

were

where

the	our
they	your
they're	you're
there	here
their	hear

for	we
four	me
do	he
due	she
I	see

yes	are
no	was
you	a
saw	all
said	so

Intermediate phonics terms, defined
(This page is an overview for the teacher/parent.)

A **digraph** is a combination of two vowels making one sound (as in rain).

A **diphthong** is a combination of two vowels making two sounds (i.e. BOTH vowel sounds are heard distinctly: as in boil, boy)

Digraph and diphthong lists of words are covered comprehensively in reading exercises in *Alpha-Phonics*. For now, it is enough to see a quick overview of these and other further intermediate phonics.

r-controlled vowels
ir	(bird)	ur	(fur)	er	(broth-er)
or	(for)				

endings
ing	(suffix)

"y" sounding as "i" when at the end of a word (cry, fly)

3 further sounds for "a"
ar	(far)
aw	(awe)
au	(automobile)

digraphs
oo	(book)	oo	(moose)

many more digraphs were taught already in the long vowel drills in this book

diphthongs
ou/ow	(loud/cow)		oy	(toy)
ew	(few)		oi	(boil)

Intermediate phonics overview

(Use this page and the next two pages to introduce the child to these new sounds. Say the sound and the phrase; have him repeat them both after you.)

ou/ow (as in **ou**ch, l**ou**d / c**ow**, h**ow**)

oy (t**oy**)

oo (b**oo**k, l**oo**k--m**oo**, ch**oo**se)

ing (s**ing**)

y (cr**y**, fl**y**) (sounds like the long "i" at the end of a word)

er (broth**er**)

ew (f**ew**)   **ir** (b**ir**d)

ar (c**ar**, f**ar**)   **or** (f**or**)

aw (**aw**e)   **ur** (f**ur**)

au (**au**tomobile)

167

Fun memory hooks
for some irregular decodings

Have the child memorize each diphthong's silly phrase.
Then test them, in random order.

ir   The th**ir**d b**ir**d tw**ir**led and
sw**ir**led around the g**ir**l.

ur   The animal of f**ur**
had an abs**ur**d p**ur**r !   #@&*+!

ar   The st**ar** c**ar** got stuck in the t**ar**.

ew   He fl**ew** a f**ew** feet.

ow   The c**ow** pl**ow**ed d**ow**nt**ow**n.

ou   Sh**ou**t a l**ou**d "**ou**ch"!

oo   When we l**oo**ked in the
b**oo**k, the m**oo**se and
the g**oo**se were on the
l**oo**se.

aw and au

We s**aw** an **aw**esome **au**tomobile.

oy and oi

The stolen t**oy**
made the b**oy**
b**oi**l!

Meet the "er" family:

moth-**er**
fath-**er**
sist-**er**
broth-**er**
dog **er** cat
and an aunt **er** uncle **er** 2!

ing   Sing the end-**ing**!

y   When "y's" are at the end of a word,
they cr**y**, "Oh m**y**"!

Flashcards of the diphthongs on these two pages are
available for purchase from HomeschoolHowTos.com

Fun story using irregular vowels and diphthongs

(Help your child read this page, as a summation of what has been learned.)

Ouch, **ou**ch, m**y** broth**er**! You s**ing** so l**ou**d, it makes me want to fl**y ou**tside, so I will not cr**y**! Wh**y** not be like m**y** t**oy** c**ar**, which p**ur**rs like a b**ir**d? A f**ew** more sh**ou**ts will make me go f**ar** away from t**o**wn for a f**ew** weeks. I will br**ing** m**y aw**esome b**oo**k ab**ou**t a l**oo**se g**oo**se and a l**oo**se m**oo**se, and there the l**ou**d s**ou**nds will be no more. S**ing** with**ou**t b**oi**ling, my broth**er**, s**ing** j**oy**fully.

Fast Phonics Certificate of Completion

Date: _____, _____

I, _____

can read! I am able to:

✓ Read and say all 26 letters, a to z.

✓ Read and say simple 2- and 3- letter short vowel words.

✓ Read and say some of the most common sight words, long vowel sounds, blends and diphthongs.

Future steps

The alphabet song

If you have already used the alphabet song by substituting phonetic sounds for the alphabet names (as per the prior suggestion on the song's page early in this book), you may now go ahead and teach it again using the alphabet NAMES.

If and when you do get ready to teach it the traditional way, you might want to change the ending words a bit to replace the rather demanding tone of "Tell me what you think of me." You could choose either of these endings: "Next time won't you sing with me?" or "Happy, happy I will be!"

Alpha-Phonics

For reinforcement and to increase fluency, you can now breeze through Samuel Blumenfeld's excellent book, *Alpha-Phonics*. It is a thin, slim 8 ½ x 11" book, superbly organized, containing lists and lists of very controlled vocabulary that increase in complexity, ever so subtly. It is a marvelous easy next step. With your *Fast Phonics* foundation, you'll race through it in no time and your young reader's fluency will increase markedly. This completes your full phonics tutoring.

Congratulations!

You have given your child one of the greatest gifts you could ever give a child, as efficiently as possible, in the shortest amount of time. He or she can now go unlock that big-wide world.

A letter from Renée

Dear Parent/Teacher,

When undertaking any new endeavor, ***beginnings are everything***. If foundations aren't secured well, the entire edifice can eventually collapse, given enough time and pressure. And so it is with reading instruction. Since reading is the first and most important academic challenge the child will ever undertake, it is of paramount importance that the process be handled with utmost care. It must end in success.

For an adult, reading can be a daily joy (as is the case with voracious readers) or a source of repeated embarrassment (as is the case with the functionally illiterate who live in a private daily nightmare). When the poor reader (we as a nation graduate millions of these) is forced to read aloud in public, all too often his halting, broken reading repeatedly dive-bombs his core identity and self-respect. And what we lose as a nation when a large percentage of our citizenry cannot comprehend basic instruction manuals, prescription drug cautions, insurance forms, public signage and application forms is incalculable.

Sadly, due to our poor reading instruction as a nation, for too long now, we sit below about 24 other countries in national reading scores. And this, from the most prosperous and progressive nation in the world.

Fast Phonics is now sent into the fray and chaos to help reverse all of this. It is a new solution to help halt our nation's academic downward spiral. This tightly designed advanced method succeeds in eliminating scores of possibilities for falling behind, or for suffering feelings of intimidation, or an inability to "keep up," or feelings of inferiority—even along the way. With *Fast Phonics*, "I CAN" is the child's constant companion. The student begins with "I DO read each new step" and ends up with "I can READ — I *get* this!"

You now have a tool in your hands that can help your loved ones, who have yet to learn to read, join the ranks of people who can read well and now can get there with remarkable speed.

If you liked Fast Phonics, try
Zoom-Type and Quick Piano!

✓ Fast. Easy. Fun.
✓ Save time (no taxiing to lessons), money (no expensive lessons) and stress ('tis self-taught!)
✓ Learned with pictures, in step by step small successful progressions, via quick spaced repetition

Both courses are totally portable. You'll happily tap your way to typing and piano-playing competency.

Zoom-Type is learned in five days!

Quick Piano teaches easy chords so that you can begin playing with a full sound right away.

Both courses are good for ages 4 to 94

Start now and you'll soon WOW your friends!

http://homeschoolhowtos.com

Made in the USA
Middletown, DE
14 March 2019

HOMESCHOOL HOW-TO'S
Renée Ellison

Razor Sharp Tips for Homeschool Moms

homeschoolhowtos.com   Email: info@homeschoolhowtos.com

"Your materials are like brain candy to me." (Mother of 6 in Iowa)

"I think your recent motherhood tips are near masterpieces. Your articles have always been meaty, but these recent ones beat all." (Mother of 5 in Virginia)

Inspiration by a professional award-winning teacher and veteran homeschooler:

- **Over 100 how-to books, booklets, e-books/Kindle books, including:**
    + Keyboarding courses: *Quick Piano* and *Zoom-Type*
    + *Teachers' Secrets & Motherhood Savvy for Homeschoolers*
    + *Razor Sharp Teaching Tips for Homeschool Moms*
    + *Wise Womanly Ways to Grow Your Marriage*

- **New release this year: *Fast Phonics: The Easy Track to Reading*** *"This method clicks and sticks!"*

- **Over 140 podcasts – more than 80 hours –on a portable, reusable 8GB jump drive for easy access**

- **Motherhood blogs on homeschool topics**

See order form (other side of this sheet) for all the titles.
Visit homeschoolhowtos.com website for product descriptions, tables of contents, and free samples.

Renee's HOMESCHOOL HOW-TO's order form (rev.6/2017)

Name: _____

Street, City/State/ZIP: _____

Phone: (____) ____ - ____ Email: _____

*note an E in Qty. if you want this as an **ebook** or **K** for **Kindle** (you pay no shipping)

(prices listed are for the print version)
(please note quantity if other than 1)
(⇐ print clearly!)
(page references are to full catalog)

Item#	Title (and full catalog page number)	Price	Qty.	Cost
all	**One-of-Each Special Deal** (p. 16)	$350.00		$
PDF	**One-of-Each E-Books Deal** (p. 16)	$205.00		$
1	Zoom-Type (includes audio CD) (p. 2)	$29.95		$
1N	Speedy 10-Key (p. 2)	$5.00		$
1N	Hebrew Zoom-Type (p. 2)	$15.95		$
2	Quick Piano (p. 2)	$5.00		$
2D	Quick Piano (includes audio CD) (p. 2)	$29.95		$
2D	Quick Piano demonstration DVD (p. 2)	$7.99		$
3	**Zoom-Type and Quick Piano** (p. 2) *Save $12*	$47.90		$
4	Goal Setting & Time Management (p. 10)	$2.00		$
5	Critical Thinking Skills (p. 6)	$5.50		$
6	Financial Steps/Money (p. 10) K$3.50; E$4.50	$5.50		$
7	12 Amazing Brain Triggers (p. 4) K$2.99 E$3.50	$4.50		$
8	Homeschooling-Gifted Child (p. 5) K$2.99; E$2.50	$3.50		$
9	Motivation: Academic Energizer (p. 5)	$2.00		$
13	Rindercella (included in #s 25 & 51) (p. 6) (ebook)	$1.50		$
14	Famous People Who Homeschooled (p. 5)	$1.50		$
15	Smart Study Skills (p. 5) Kindle $.99; ebook $1.50	$2.00		$
16	Training Children Further (p. 7)	$3.50		$
17	Sure-fire Penmanship (included in #81) (p. 4)	$1.00		$
18	Woman: God's Design (p. 9) Kin. $2.99; ebook $4	$4.50		$
19	Beyond Discipline (p. 7) K $4.99; ebook $3	$3.50		$
20	Rooms / Message: Interior Design (p. 10)	$3.50		$
21	Dinner: The Stage and the Drama (p. 10)	$3.50		$
22	I Have To Fix Dinner Again?! (p.10) K:Ebk $2.99	$3.50		$
23	Feminine Dress (p. 9)	$2.50		$
24	**Teach Math Faster** (p. 6) K $4.99; ebook $3	$3.50		$
25	Goofy Little Rewards (p. 5) Ebk $2.50; Ki. or print	$2.99		$
26	**Character Traits book, & songs CD: NIV or KJV?** (p. 7)	**$15.00**		$
26CDs	Character Traits songs & PDF text files 2-CDs (p. 7)	**$15.00**		$
26S	Character Traits songs audio CD (p. 7)	$5.99		$
27S	Character Traits book extras: **NIV or KJV?** (p. 7)	$11.00		$
28	Lost Treasures from Men of Character (p. 8)	$12.00		$
29	Teach Children Bible Doctrine (p.7) Data CD or prt.	$5.00		$
30	Party Themes and Activities (p. 11)	$5.00		$
31	Keep Kids from Materialism (p. 11) K$.99; Ebk $2	$3.00		$
32	TV Watching Out of Control (p. 12)	$3.00		$
34	Drive 'n Shine Car Detailing Manual (p. 8)	$5.00		$
36	Challenge for Graduating Seniors (p. 9)	$5.00		$
37	Godly Daughter Checklist (p. 8) Kin.$2.99; E$2.50	$1.50		$
38a	Godly Son Checklist (p. 8) Kindle $2.99; Ebk $2.50; E$2.99	$2.99		$
38b	Wesley's Holiness Checklist (p. 8)	$2.99		$
39	Sharing the Birds and the Bees (p. 12)	$2.99		$
40	Creation vs. Evolution (included in #51) (p. 6)	$1.00		$
41	Christ and His Birth: Object Lessons (p. 11)	$1.00		$
42	Got Off the Christmas Bandwagon (p. 11) Kindle $.99	$2.50		$
43	Jewish Holidays Made Simple (p. 11) (free ebook)	$3.50		$
44	Family Road Trips Humor (p. 12) K$2.99; E$5.50	$2.00		$
45	Tips on How to Write a Play (p. 7)	$3.50		$
46	Raising an Only Child (p. 7)	$3.50		$
47	How Not to Waste Your Youth (p. 8) K$.99 E$2	$2.50		$
48	Life of J. S. Bach (also get #89)(p. 13) K$.99; E$2.50	$2.00		$
49	Bach stage play (per script; cast of 10+) (p. 13)	$3.50		$
50	Speak with Ease (p. 13)	$5.00		$
51	Academic Checklist (includes #s 13 & 41) (p.6) K/E $2.99	$5.00		$
52	Humpty Dumpty Intellectual Stretch (in #8)(p. 5)	$1.00		$
53	Teach Children to Draw (p. 13) Kindle/E $.99	$1.50		$
54	Grandparenting (+#9) (p. 12) Kin. $.99; Ebk $1.50	$1.50		$
55		$1.50		$

Item#	Title (and full catalog page number)	Price	Qty.	Cost
56	Cultivate Lasting Love of the Bible (p.7) K/E $.99	$2.50		$
57	No Stress Holidays for Moms (p. 11)	$2.00		$
58	Turbo-charged Nutrition (p. 10) K$2.99; Ebk $3.95	$5.50		$
59	Me? Keep the Sabbath? (p. 11) (free ebook) Kin.$.99	$2.00		$
60	Homeschool Advantages (p. 4) K$.99; Ebk $2.99	$3.50		$
61	Avoid Homeschool Burnout (p. 4) K$2.99 E$2.50	$3.00		$
62	Miscarriage (p. 12)	$2.50		$
63	Preserve & Arrange Family Papers (p. 11)	$2.50		$
64	Survival for Simpletons (p. 11) (Kindle/ebook $3.99)	$5.50		$
65	Biblical Tassels: Thoughts about Tzitziot (p. 8)	$2.00		$
66	Ten Extraordinary Stories…Debt-free (p. 10)	$5.00		$
67	Common Pitfalls in Homeschooling (p. 4) K$2.99	$3.50		$
68	The Biblical Headcovering (p. 9) (free Ebk) K$.99	$4.00		$
69	Homeschooling a Resistant Child (p. 4) K$2.99 E$2.50	$3.50		$
70	Waiting for Mr. Right (p. 8) K$.99 ebook $2.50	$3.00		$
71	Men Preparing for Marriage (p. 8) K$.99 EB$2.50	$3.00		$
72	Home Management (p. 10) Kindle or ebook $3.95	$5.50		$
73	Let a Woman Keep Silent/ Assembly (p. 9)	$2.00		$
74	Controlling Person (p. 12) Kin. $.99; eBook $2.50	$3.50		$
75	Rembrandt: Held by God (p. 13) K$.99 Ebk$2.50	$3.00		$
76	Be Still, My Soul (audio CD) (p. 13)	$15.00		$
77	Sarah's Beauty Secret (p. 9)	$1.50		$
78	Mostly Raw Recipe Ideas (p. 9)	$3.50		$
79	Teach Grammar Faster (p. 6) K$2.99; ebook $2.50	$2.99		$
80	Training Terrific Tots (Preschool) (p. 5) K$2.99 E$4.50	$5.50		$
81	The Right Stuff (p. 4) (incl.#s 17, 52 & 83) K$2.99	$4.50		$
82	Dickens' *A Child's History of England* audio (p. 6)	$25.00		$
83	Ignite the Love of Writing (is in #81) (p. 4)	$2.00		$
84	Ethel Barrett's Bible Stories on CD (p. 12)	$5.99		$
85	D. L. Moody; as told by Ethel Barrett (p. 12)	$5.99		$
88	Self-induced Stress (p. 12) Kindle or ebook $2.99	$3.75		$
89	Bach & Rembrandt biographies audio CD (p. 13)	$5.99		$
90	In Better Arms than These Lullabies CD (p. 13)	$5.99		$
95	Discipline Strategies for Groups (DVD) (p.3)	$6.99		$
96	Power of a Focused Mother (p. 9) Kin. $2.99	$2.99		$
98	Child Training Tips bundle (#s 16, 19, 95)	$14.00		$
100	Sewing Basics (p. 7) Kindle $2.99; eBook $2.50	$3.50		$
105	Homeschooling To-Do Charts (p.5) K$2.99; E$2.50	$3.50		$
106	Spell-Along! (spelling lists + audio CD) (p. 5)	$7.50		$
107	Master a Musical Instrument (p. 13) K$2.99; E$2.50	$3.50		$
108	Home Staging Tips (p. 10) Kindle/ebook $.99	$2.00		$
109	In Dire Straits? How to rescue finances (p. 10)	$5.00		$
110	Motherhood Tips (choose booklet or audio CD) (p. 13)	$5.00		$
111	Melanie's Favorite Books List (p. 6) (free ebook)	$2.50		$
113	**Teachers' Secrets/Motherhood Savvy** (p. 13) K$9.95	$14.95		$
114	**Wise Womanly Ways/Grow Marriage** (p.9) (K$7.50)	$9.95		$
115	**Fast Phonics** 180-page course book (pages 6 and 14)	$29.95		$
116	Fast Phonics **Letter Cartoons** 48-page book	$15.00		$
116	Fast Phonics **Heavy Duty Portable Letter Charts**	$15.00		$
116	Fast Phonics **Power Pac Duo Flashcard** set	$15.00		$
116	Fast Phonics **Diphthong Picture Flashcards**	$8.00		$
117	Hebrew Alef-Bet for Simpletons (p. 2) (ebook $2.00)	$5.50		$
119	Kindergarten Songs & Rhythms (audio CD)	$5.99		$
120	**Razor Sharp Teaching Tips** (illustrated; p.4) E or K $4.99	$9.95		$
121	Renée's audio how-to's (80+ hours/8GB USB drive) (p.3)	$19.95		$
	Catalog of all our products (**free—just ask for it!**)			

Order total (payable **online** at Homeschoolhowtos.com by credit card or PayPal, by **phone** with credit card, or by **check** to Cross-Over)

Sub-totals: **(left-hand column):** $ _____ . _____

(right-hand column): $ _____ . _____

Add 2.9% state sales tax for sales within Colorado; _____ . _____

Shipping and handling is 10% (minimum charge $3.50; maximum charge $15.00); + _____ . _____

= **Product sub-total:** _____ . _____

= **Order total:** $ _____ . -0-

Mailing address: **HOMESCHOOL HOW-TO'S**, 190 Vista Linda Ave., Durango, CO 81303
Make checks payable to Cross-Over.
Phone: 1-970-385-1809 (Mon.-Fri.; we accept credit card orders over the phone)
Email: Info@homeschoolhowtos.com **Website:** www.homeschoolhowtos.com